The Art of

Problem Solving

The Art of
Problem Solving

How to Improve Your Methods

by

EDWARD HODNETT

HARPER & ROW, PUBLISHERS

NEW YORK, EVANSTON, AND LONDON

Library of Congress catalog card number: 55–8554

To

Jessie

Contents

CONTENTS

Acknowledgments

I am indebted to many sources for information and examples too incidental to justify footnotes or bibliography in an untechnical book of this sort. I thank the authors and editors.

The manuscript benefited substantially from the criticisms of Victor A. Goedicke, Paul M. Kendall, George T. Le Boutillier, R. B. McAdoo, Charles Allen Smart, Ordway Tead, and Marian Tyndall. I am happy to acknowledge my debt and my gratitude.

E. H.

The Art of

Problem Solving

1

You and Your Problems

PROBLEM solving is everybody's problem. Whether you are a housewife, a druggist, a secretary, a student, a filling-station operator, a business executive, or the man who lives in the White House, you have to solve problems. Fortunately, human beings like to solve problems. Otherwise how can you explain people who play chess, climb mountains, and offer to open folding bridge tables?

As an intelligent citizen with personal, professional, and community responsibilities, you face the usual variety of problems. You may wish to smoke less, eat less, spend less, worry less, or be loved more. You may have to decide whether to accept a promotion and move to Syracuse, or stay in Omaha. You may have a daughter who wishes to marry a traveling man or a son who wishes to be a disk jockey. You may have to bid on a contract, market a new product, set up a new wage scale, redecorate your house, or fire a cook. You have to vote on bond issues for roads and schools, consider remedies for juvenile delinquency, and take your stand on national and international policies. You have lots of problems.

Problem solving is so important I believe it ought to be studied all by itself. It rarely is. People who are skilled in solving problems in one field too seldom apply a systematic approach to problems outside their field. Yet the problems of medicine, mining, and merchan-

1

dising are much alike in structure, and they respond to much the same techniques of solution. And since techniques can be learned, you can improve your methods of problem solving and so add to your daily efficiency and to your enjoyment of life.

The Art of Problem Solving aims at helping you to improve your methods for all your problems, not just one specialized type. Problems are not solved by any one system or by rigid one-two-three methods. Each chapter, therefore, deals with a different aspect of problem solving. This approach puts less strain on you than a textbook organization, where the chapters progress in a logical sequence and mastery of one is prerequisite to undertaking the next. You can read *The Art of Problem Solving* in a more relaxed manner and put it down and pick it up again without being lost.

The chapters fall into four groups. Part I presents aspects of the important initial phase—*Diagnosis.* Part II deals with the other main phase—various aspects of the *Attack* that follows your diagnosis. These are common techniques applicable to any of your problems. Part III makes a fresh start. You might say that you are now interested in how you think about the methods you use for diagnosis and attack. This emphasis on systematic reasoning gives you the simplest aspects of the *Scientific Approach.* These chapters enable you to exert more rigorous control over your problem-solving efforts. In Part IV you look at the whole question from a new point of view. You consider those aspects that make problem solving an *Art* as well as a science.

You will find in each chapter an abundance of examples because they are the shortest bridge between theory and reality, and I hope you will find plenty of parallels to your own problems. Unless otherwise indicated, all the examples are real, though sometimes disguised and simplified.

At the end of each chapter are suggestions for applying the points discussed to your past and present problems. By making this application chapter by chapter you will derive immediate benefit from your reading. Whether you do this alone or with associates concerned with the same kind of problems, you will be pursuing a personal course of study. You will also assimilate the sense of each chapter better with this periodic review than you would if you read right along. At least stop at the end of each chapter to go back over the main ideas and to check them against one or two of your own problems. And take a breather after each group of chapters for reflection and rest. If you are to use *The Art of Problem Solving* in a practical way, you will need time to mull over the ideas and examples as you go along. Do not be alarmed to find so many aspects of problem solving discussed. To be understood thoroughly, any complex activity must be broken down into a number of smaller units. But you do not try to carry all of these separate items in your head and put them into effect one after the other when you engage in the activity. You can count on that wonderful mechanism your brain to store, combine, select, and produce the information you need—if there has been solid input in the first place. Then in time it will correct its own errors.

The Art of Problem Solving covers the same ground more than once. But if you come at the same conclusions from a number of angles, remember that the truth has many faces. Or you might say that problem solving is much like eating an apple—to get at the core, you have to bite an apple from all sides. If you are patient, you should be able to develop a pattern in your thinking about all kinds of problems. Establishing patterns of thinking—reducing problem solving to habits of mind—is standard scientific procedure. In *How We Think* John Dewey describes the following steps: (1) perplexity—an awareness of the problem; (2) analysis and clarification by observation and reflection—definition of the problem; (3) consideration of different solutions or working hypotheses for solution of the problem; (4) verification of the solution chosen. Perhaps in time you can reduce your efforts to this classic simplicity.

What is a problem? Essentially is it not a state of disorder? Suppose the ocean is cutting into the bluff on which your summer cot-

3

tage stands. That area of your life occupied by ownership of the cottage is unsettled. To bring it back to an equilibrium, to a state of order, you must make a decision and take action. Can you hold back the sea somehow? No. Can you move the house? Yes. Can you do anything else? Yes. You might sell the house. What will happen if you do nothing? You will lose your house.

You seem to have a choice of moving your cottage or of selling it. If you make a satisfactory decision, then the thoughts and activities that revolve about your summer cottage will settle down. Like a child's building blocks that have been scattered and then rearranged in a square of alternating colors, your affairs concerned with the cottage regain an organization, a pattern. The solving of problems is the search for order, for the overcoming of disorder.

Recognizing problems is not always simple. You will often start with only the recognition that you have a *problem situation*. There is something wrong with your health. You are tired all the time. That is a typical problem situation. Until what is wrong is spotted, the problem is not clear enough to solve. But seeing that a problem situation exists is a step toward finding the problem and solving it.

What is a solution? Solutions are not bricks—neat and much alike. One solution will be complete, nearly perfect. Another will be incomplete, but the best that you can work out. Except in mathematical problems, a solution rarely if ever equals *the* answer. It is the one that you have chosen as the *best* in the circumstances. Another might work better. Under other circumstances you might choose another. Still, while you look for the best answer for a specific problem at a specific time, you hope to find one that will work for similar problems in the future.

Few problems have entirely satisfactory solutions. My house is built on the downslope of a steep hill. I cannot solve the problem of a garage for my car. There is no space for a garage. But I have improved the situation. With a buttress of logs, a few loads of fill, and a brick surface I have created an area where I can park my car off the street. Solving a problem does not necessarily mean wiping it out. It often means ameliorating it—making it less troublesome to live with. By freeing yourself from the obsessive drive to reach perfect solutions, you will find all your problems—and yourself—easier to live with.

To a person trained in a technical discipline, the methods advocated here may seem too simplified. Building a bridge unquestionably requires the solving of technical problems by engineers trained in mysteries such as indeterminate structures. But bridges are not built by engineers alone. Taxpayers, city officials, newspaper editors, and other spokesmen for the public decide that the bridge is to be built, what kind it is to be, where it is to be, what it will cost, and how it will be paid for. Decision making in a democracy and in most business and other organizations is rarely left to the technician alone. Though the number of specialists in our society has passed counting, the main role of the specialist is that of a consultant. For the broad activity of decision making, you will find a broad approach is necessary.

These remarks are not meant as a discourtesy to those patient and brilliant people who work out their problems in university studies, in consultants' offices, and in modern laboratories equipped with precision instruments. What you might take over from the scientist— and what the scientist might apply to problems outside his specialty —is the habit of approaching problems in an organized way. Problem solving is not merely the search for order. It is the establishment and cultivation of order once it is discovered. Only in that portion of the universe that has been subjected to some degree of order can future events be reliably predicted.

Scientist and layman, we are all tied to logic. We can range only as far as our reason extends. The manipulation of mathematical symbols, chemical formulas, and the other paraphernalia of the scientist has little meaning unless it is dominated by rigorous logic. But for your purposes rigorous need not mean complicated. We shall therefore try to use the principal logical processes without becoming lost in formal logic.

Problems are complex. Easy-answer people cause more problems than they solve. Many problems are not merely complex. They are in reality complexes—groups of problems put under one heading for convenience of reference. "The problem of Germany" will be worked out only by multitudes of decisions and actions in regard to many distinct problems. Large problems are settled by solving the smaller ones of which they are composed. Large problems can rarely be solved in any other way. For instance, the efforts of the women of the city of Bremen to adopt the methods of our P.T.A. and League of Women Voters will have some bearing on how far Germany turns toward democracy.

Problems change. Even as you study a problem, it changes. Your efforts to solve it will change it. Your progress in understanding problem solving in general, as well as your progress in understanding a specific problem, will change that problem and the next one like it. As a result of the complexity and variability of problems, you adopt another basic position—that the principle of relativity applies in a high degree to human affairs. Your search for order is not a search for absolutes. The beliefs men hold are not subject to measurement, and even in the technical fields it is clear that truth is subject to change.

Your command of predictability and your confidence will increase as you attack your problems in a systematic, rational manner. You will feel more confident when you no longer rely on optimism and opportunism. Even being able to predict which problems you are not likely to solve is good for your peace of mind. Certain problems have specialized backgrounds with which you may not be familiar; others are stubborn and have hardened from long standing; and some are controlled by forces over which you have no power. You need feel no qualms about letting such problems ride for a while. But by increasing

6

your understanding of the ways to go about subduing problems, you increase the number you can subdue.

You can increase your skill in growing dahlias, playing poker, and investing money. If you can improve in these activities and a host of others, you can increase your proficiency in solving problems. As you sharpen your wits in dealing with the different aspects of problem solving, you respond with eagerness to the challenge of a new problem. Through patience and practice you will master the moves in what is one of the most fascinating games and one of the most useful arts.

* * *

Consider your own education and experience. How much instruction in problem solving have you received? Have you been taught to solve only certain kinds of problems? Or have you developed systematic procedures for solving all kinds of problems? What is your definition of a problem? How much practical value you derive from *The Art of Problem Solving* depends on how diligently you apply your reading to your own problems. Therefore my first suggestion is that you make a thoughtful record of your problems. Put each one on a separate card, on a separate page in a notebook, or in a separate folder, so that you can add ideas as they occur to you. Then you will have readily available for practical application a file of your past and current problems. The past problems will be useful to analyze because they provide complete histories, including early hypotheses, trial solutions, and final results. Since past problems may recur, their analysis is not academic. Your file of current problems will give you a chance to apply your reading. As you consider each aspect of problem solving, you can make direct applications of practical benefit to you.

Part I

DIAGNOSIS

IN THIS section you are dealing with various aspects of the first phase of problem solving—diagnosis. As in medicine, diagnosis aims at making clear the exact nature of the trouble. The six chapters do not represent six steps that you take in the order they are printed. Your diagnosis of almost any problem will blend these six considerations as inseparably as the ingredients of a cocktail. Still, your well-mixed diagnosis will contain an *Identification* and a *Statement* of the problem. It will require an *Analysis*, which must get much of its value from the shrewdness of the *Questions* you raise. And, of course, straightening out your *Facts* and *Assumptions* is an important part of your diagnosis. In many problems you have little more to do once you have made a sound diagnosis.

2

Identification

Eagerness to solve a problem—or to punch somebody in the nose—before the problem has been properly identified accounts for much of the inefficiency and grief associated with the vast human activity of problem solving. Your first act as a practicing problem solver is to hold everything until you have disentangled your problem from the general problem situation that enfolds and often obscures it.

The office manager in one of the branches of your business tells you that she is thinking of quitting because she is being unfairly overworked. She implies that you are responsible for her troubles. As her boss, in a way you are. But you resent the hostility and the inference that you are indifferent to the welfare of your employees. In short order you could be embroiled in a bootless wrangle. Instead, you try to isolate the specific problem in the general situation. You are willing to concede that the manager has too much to do, if she says she has. But you cannot work on that alone. After a while she clarifies the situation as follows: The growth in the volume of business at that branch has increased her load and particularly her personnel duties. She finally identifies her problem more exactly in this way: "Personnel has grown too big for me to handle along with my other work." Your solution is then clear. You give her an assistant to take care of personnel and to help her in other ways.

Your problems do not usually come in packages all ready to solve.

11

As in the case above, you generally start on a something-is-wrong basis. Or you start with what seems the problem but later proves not to be. A resolute determination to take no action until you are sure you have identified your problem is therefore your first contribution toward its solution.

Distinguishing between the problem situation and the problem itself is only the first of your efforts at identification. You face two other tasks. You have to identify the *real* problem, and you have to identify the *total* problem. Doubtless more than once you have complimented yourself on your admirable efforts to solve a problem—only to discover that it is not the problem you should have solved or that it is merely part of a larger unsolved problem.

Nat and Katherine Ellis have been quarreling recently about domestic problems—whether they should send Elaine to a country-day school, whether they can afford to trade in their car, whether they should go to his mother's or hers for Christmas. The Ellises are devoted to one another. What really troubles Nat is the fear that Katherine may have to undergo a serious operation. What upsets Katherine is that Nat looks worried and acts unhappy. She is afraid that perhaps he is dissatisfied with his marriage.

Finally Nat and Katherine talk things over. They recognize that the real problem is Katherine's health. That problem cannot be disposed of by direct action, except to see that Katherine receives proper medical care. But the Ellises are able to clear up the marginal problems and ameliorate the main one by understanding that it is their one real problem and by facing it together.

Why do we fail to see the real problem? The reason is sometimes sheer blindness. Sometimes the real problem is so hidden behind foreground problems or is so tangled up in its own ramifications or is so hedged by technicalities that only patience, high intelligence, or special training can penetrate to it. But the commonest reason is emotional bias. We drop the belladonna of prejudice, fear, cupidity, preconceived notions, conceit, or partisan loyalty into our eyes. Then we see only what our emotional bias allows us to see. If Arnold is involved in a problem and Barlow dislikes Arnold, the film of prejudice slips over Barlow's eyes and what he sees is not the problem that Arnold raises. Or if Barlow is Arnold's friend and a problem seems in any way to include factors adversely affecting Arnold, Barlow transforms the problem into his problem—the defense of Arnold, no matter what comes up.

The Morgenthau plan for treating the Germans after World War II set out to prevent the Germans from ever waging war again. The Morgenthau plan would have solved this problem. It would have dismantled Germany's industry, the sinews of war, and turned her into an agricultural nation. But Germany has thirty million people more than she can feed. Until that vast number had died off, the Morgenthau plan would not work—and long before then the Germans would have gone over to the Russians. The real problem is how to prevent the Germans from ever waging war against us again, and yet to rebuild themselves as an industrial nation able to take care of themselves and to contribute to the welfare and stability of the world. Morgenthau's hatred of the war-making Prussians and Nazis blinded him to the real problem. His solution, therefore, was no solution.

Another basic difficulty in seeing the real problem is that it often exists in the future. It is not part of the present situation. The present situation is fluid, developing, and the real problem therefore has still to take shape in the future. Since this is the meat of the problem solving of experienced administrators, they often take a dim view of the solutions directed only at the problems under the solvers' noses. The guests at a remote resort hotel may offer excellent suggestions about improving the service. The real problem to the management may be how to secure enough competent help to keep operating. Editorial writers and isolationist politicians may object to granting financial aid to a certain foreign country. To the President the real problem may not be whether or not to give aid, but whether or not, even with our aid, the friendly government of that country can keep in office and so keep the country on our side.

Your skill as a problem solver includes more than the ability to see that there is a problem in a situation. You must distinguish the real problem from the apparent ones. Then your identification of the problem becomes part of the solution.

What you take to be *the* problem is often only part of a larger one. You have to deal with the *total* problem.

Gus Stevens was a good printer—experienced, conscientious, resourceful. He had many friends in Nashtown who assured him of plenty of business if he set up his own firm. But Gus was cautious. He had seen too many small businesses fold up to want to repeat their mistakes. He figured that the main reason for their failure— apart from lack of experience and too much competition—was insufficient capital and too elaborate a start. Gus bided his time until he had ample capital, bought a small plant with new linotype and photo-offset presses, and started in business on a modest scale.

Gus stuck it out for two and a half years. Then he sold out for a little less than he had paid for the business and went back to working for a big plant. What Gus discovered was that there was more to running a printing business than he could handle. He could do a good job of printing, if he only could stay in the shop long enough. He could get the business all right, if only he had the time to get out and hustle and be available to talk over jobs with clients. Then there was the paper work. Gus had never realized how specialized the cost accounting of printing is. If he figured a bit too high, he did not get the job. If he figured a bit too low, he was working without pay. And there were the government forms to fill out. If he ignored a single form or filled it in inaccurately, he spent double time straightening himself out.

Gus Stevens failed to size up his total problem in the first place. Gus considered printing a technical process. He underestimated sales, promotion, accounting, and general office management. He could

14

not solve his whole problem. Every year many thousands of men and women fail in business for the same reason.

Here is a common family problem. Your daughter Mildred announces that she has been asked to go to the high-school Junior prom at the country club with breakfast at 6:00 A.M. at somebody's house. You cannot handle this problem on a simple yes-or-no basis. You have to take a look at the total problem first. You must consider at least two larger aspects before your reaction to the immediate problem has much value. First you have to see that your whole relationship with your daughter is involved. She is growing up. This occasion is important to her. An arbitrary decision from you might damage your relations in other matters. Second, you cannot pry Mildred's problem loose from the total problem of what all the kids are doing these days. If you refuse to let her go on the assumption that it is not the kind of occasion a nice girl should attend, you may be depriving her of a memorable evening of innocent fun and of sharing in a ritual of her teen-age group. If some of your fears are justified, you still may be doing more harm than good by not letting her face her own problems. Yet if you agree to let her go without examining the situation, you may be acquiescing in conditions that are thoroughly unsatisfactory.

You may wonder about formulating problems that are not presented in their entirety when first you meet them. Many of them literally cannot be. They unfold step by step over a period of time. Since the parts are not presented in a sequence having any particular logic, you may well wonder how you can grasp the total problem. The answer is that you cannot. All that you can grasp is a *concept* of the total problem as it appears to you at a given time. It is therefore of the greatest importance that you reshape and restate the total problem just as often as developments warrant. The record of our varying policy toward the Russians is an example of how activity on a tremendous scale may be controlled by an almost day-by-day reshaping of what appears to be the total problem.

The survival of a business or other enterprise demands the ability to see the total problem as it is projected in a changing, dynamic form. I once became an enthusiastic user of a certain electronic office machine during its trial development period. It was lighter, cheaper, and better than any other I had used. I was certain that with some technical improvements it would supersede its rivals. To my astonishment the president of the company told me that the machine would not go into production.

"We weren't worried about technical problems," he explained. "But when we examined the financial standing of the two big leaders in the field, we discovered that the first was $500,000 in the red and the other was carrying an inventory of $7,000,000—a ruinous situation in case of an international crisis. Our problem is not to design machines that will operate successfully. Our problem is to design machines that can also be sold for a profit."

Just as you cannot always grasp all of the parts of a problem at once, neither can you always present the total concept of a complex problem to another at once. You cannot do it instantaneously; you often cannot do it in one meeting. You therefore have to be patient in presenting each step to summarize where you are in relation to the whole. Your listener or reader should not lose sight of the gist of the total problem. When you are on the receiving end of the presentation, you will conserve time and energy—and avoid making a fool of yourself—if you will suspend judgment until the presentation is complete and you are sure you grasp the whole problem. Suspension of judgment and decision until then is desirable because the other person often fails to see the total problem he is talking about. It is then up to you to supply the vision that he lacks.

Keeping always before you a sense of the relatedness of the parts to the whole problem is an act of synthesis. Whether you function as a chief executive or someone far down the line, your job is always to make your efforts contribute to the solution of the problem as a whole. Failure to grasp the total problem makes an executive worthless. Failure on the part of a subordinate can mean that a well-intentioned man works to solve individual problems without contributing to the solution of the whole problem—he may even be pulling in the wrong direction.

You start your diagnosis of a problem by identifying it. First you separate it from the general problem situation in which it usually makes its first appearance. Next you distinguish the real problem from the apparent ones. Then you relate the immediate problem to the total problem of which it is sometimes only a part. You are now ready to go on to the statement of your problem and to further aspects of the diagnosis.

• • •

Using hindsight, state on the record of each of your past problems (1) what the real problem was and (2) what the total problem was. Do these notes show any change in your understanding of any of your past problems? . . . Now identify the real- and total-problem aspects of your current problems. Be sure you understand the distinction between the two; then reexamine each problem. This requires more than superficial thought. Do you now believe you have identified any of your current problems more precisely?

3

Statement

❧ *Like a Christmas bauble* ☙

To DIAGNOSE a problem, you have first to put it into words or other symbols that define that problem exactly. Sometimes you will arrive at this statement quickly and easily. Sometimes you will find the hardest part of the problem is stating it. Then you know you have not yet identified it. Many business conferences go on for hours before the participants agree on exactly what problems are at the heart of their discussion. United Nations conferences on agenda—mere lists of problems for later discussion—may take weeks. The statement of a problem is essential to correct diagnosis.

You see at once that statement is only the outward form of identification. Until you have done the thinking necessary to identify your problem, you are not ready to state it. On the other hand, your probing to discover the exact nature of the problem you are dealing with is invariably carried on by words, or other symbols, as other chapters in this first section on diagnosis will show. Your effort to identify a problem, therefore, is accompanied by a simultaneous effort to find an adequate statement of it.

But the statement of a problem has importance in its own right. In a Federal Reserve bank a woman sits on a stool sorting bills according to denomination and bank of issue. She places the bills in pigeonholes spread before her for about five feet. She has been at this job for years. The officials boast about her speed. Yet the stool is

18

exactly in the center of the pigeonholes. Being right handed, she must twist her body and stretch every time she puts a low-denomination bill in one of the pigeonholes on her left. If this woman once stated her problem—how to distribute the bills as rapidly and as comfortably as possible—she would make one of the following changes: (1) put the low denomination bills, which are most numerous, on the right or possibly in the center; (2) place her stool in the center of her reach instead of in the center of the pigeonholes; (3) experiment with a revolving stool within a semicircular cabinet of pigeonholes. Until the woman frames a statement of her problem, she will never solve it efficiently.

Unless you put a problem into words, you do not give it form. If it is formless, it does not exist in a manner that permits solution. You may recognize a general problem situation, the symptoms of a problem, or one or more related problems, without stating the problem itself. There is a difference between saying to someone, "You look ill!" or "What a peculiar color your face is!" and saying, "You have jaundice." An unstated problem cannot be solved. Many problems go unsolved for centuries for lack of adequate statement.

Once you state a problem exactly, it often proves not nearly as serious as you imagined. "You will have to pay all expenses for the damage to the car" is much more alarming than "You will have to pay $28 for the damage to the car." Sometimes putting your problem into words proves you have no problem. For instance, if a sense of anxiety nags you, it will often disappear if you try to complete the sentence, "I am afraid of. . . ." If you have no grounds to fear death, disease, divorce, disgrace, or dismissal, you have reduced your anxiety to an absurdity. Before you can finish putting your problem into words, you may realize that you have been mistaken about your facts. Or perhaps your statement points to the solution—though knowing it does not necessarily make it easy to attain.

Suppose we try to arrive at a statement of the problem of Mildred and the Junior prom from the previous chapter. As Mildred first presents the problem to you, it probably registers as, "May I go to another high school dance?" Further conversation turns the word "prom" into the unaccustomed circumstances—not the high school gym but the country club where liquor is served and not until midnight but all night long, with breakfast at some vague place. You may then say, "That is no place for a girl of your age to be hanging around all night." You have identified the problem—to your own satisfaction —and pronounced judgment to boot. But if your family is a standard American model, the problem is not settled. Gradually your real problem emerges: Will you be doing your daughter more good than harm by letting her go to the prom or by refusing to let her go? Beyond this core problem circles the larger total problem. It includes social problems that might be stated as a series of propositions, such as: "Will Mildred develop more moral fiber by facing whatever hazards this situation presents than by avoiding them?" "Will our long-range relations be better if I let her make her own decision?" "How important psychologically is it to a teen-ager to conform to the customs of her group?" "What are my responsibilities for my daughter's welfare and standards?"

You may find talking a problem over with another person the best way to formulate it. Psychiatrists, guidance counselors, and others who deal professionally with personal problems base their services on first getting the patient or client to understand the nature of his trouble by putting it into words himself. Often they have to do little more. You are lucky if you have a friend or wife or associate to whom you can say, "Let me try to tell you what the Triplexo people are asking us to do, and why we can't afford to give them a flat yes or no answer." You are luckier if that person will not try to solve your problem for you but will listen closely and lead you on by asking you questions. You may find it easier to talk while you are taking a walk. In certain circumstances you will be more articulate and objective talking to someone not close to you. The freedom with which people in buses and in bars tell strangers their troubles supports this idea.

20

STATEMENT

Let these people be a warning, however, not to fall into the self-indulgence of prolonged statement of your problems. There would be many less unsolved problems if people put in half as much time trying to solve them as they do describing them.

You will find it pays to reduce your statement of a problem to writing. Business, legal, and scientific reports take the problem-and-solution form. Busy executives expect such reports as the basis for decision. If you distribute a written statement of a problem before a conference, you will save a good deal of time. Writing is more succinct than talk, and more precise. It presents the problem completely and permits it to be reviewed point by point. Imagine that you are the president of a company manufacturing milling machines. You are calling an important meeting of your top staff members to consider an urgent problem. Instead of presenting it orally, with the usual unnecessary details and digressions, you might send out beforehand a simple statement like this.

Triplexo problem:
The Triplexo Company of Pittsburgh will install our Model L-400 machine in all of their plants if we will cancel the clause in our contract giving us the right to make changes in the machine at our discretion.

Possible solutions:
1. Accept their terms.
2. Reject them.
3. Any other course of action?

In passing we hardly need say that many occasions require lengthy statements—as in legal cases, for instance. But we are talking about statements of essential problems. Even a Supreme Court decision often sums up the essence of a complex legal problem in one sentence.

Most of the chapters ahead have some bearing on the statement of your problems. But here are three definite suggestions that may be helpful from the beginning.

1. A good problem statement often includes (a) what is known,

(b) what is unknown, and (c) what is sought. For instance, the problem of Mildred and the high school prom might be restated as follows: (a) known—place, time, and importance to Mildred; (b) unknown—facts about liquor, supervision of dance, driving about in cars, and site and supervision of breakfast; (c) sought—how to have Mildred enjoy the prom without undesirable experiences. In two communities I know such a statement of this general problem led first to the discovery that the unknowns were shocking. Then the ritual of the country club and the six o'clock breakfast were preserved but with parents acting as hosts.

2. A fantastic proportion of your problems is semantic. That means that half the time you are more tangled up in words than in facts. You will therefore avoid an infinite amount of trouble by making a habit of defining with care all terms you use that might conceivably be understood in some way besides the one you mean. If, for instance, you told the woman in the Federal Reserve bank that you could help her handle her job more efficiently, she probably would reject your offer. You might be thinking mainly of her comfort, but she would not know that unless you told her. Most of the words in the dictionary have more than one literal meaning, and many have desirable and undesirable connotations. Sometimes you can fool yourself by using a word in different senses at different times. Sometimes a word like "efficiency" may have a positive flavor for you and a negative one for another person. As you consider the words in the statement of a problem, you might try Pascal's suggestion: Substitute mentally the things defined in place of the definition. Ambiguity is a cardinal sin in problem solving.

3. The way a problem is stated can block its diagnosis. Therefore in dealing with a troublesome problem it is always wise to say, "Let's state this problem over again." Restatement often brings out points omitted or overlooked the first time. Sometimes restatement in other terms—as in mathematical symbols or diagrams—will put a

problem in a fresh light. Frequent restatement of the problem is always useful. It keeps you on the target.

Statement of a solution is on occasion as important as statement of the original problem. The use of the lever must have been discovered by chance in dim antiquity. But mankind did not benefit fully until Archimedes of Syracuse two centuries before Christ stated the laws that govern the operation. Many a cook's secrets have died with her because she never wrote down her recipes—the solutions of her problems. Failure to keep historical records of original construction and subsequent changes makes repairs on large structures expensive and slow because the location of pipes, wires, and other details is not known. In scientific experiment, records of failures are as necessary as the record of success.

As a canny problem solver, then, you start out with a clear view of the problem that you are trying to solve. Problems can have many facets. Yet the ideal way to view a problem is to hold it out like a Christmas bauble and turn it round and round. That is the ideal— a clear sharp view of the problem, plain, whole, and cut off from everything else, subject to your manipulation and the probings of your intelligence. That is what you accomplish by never starting to solve a problem until you have stated it in the definite form of words, figures, pictures, or other symbols. In this process you (a) extract the problem from the general problem situation, (b) separate the real problem from the apparent ones, and (c) estimate the dimensions of the total problem that may surround the immediate one.

When you automatically refuse to consider a problem, your own or anyone else's, until it has been clearly stated, you are making progress.

•   •   •

Go over your written record of past problems. Can anyone misunderstand any of your statements? Will defining some of the terms help? Rewrite all statements that you can improve. . . . Try to improve the record of the solutions adopted for the past problems. . . . Now examine the statements of your current problems one by one. In each case have you stated the real problem, not merely the problem situation? Can you make your language more precise? Are definitions desirable? Have you distinguished between the immediate problem and the total problem surrounding it? Will figures, diagrams, or other symbols be helpful? Is your statement as concise as possible? Can you make it clearer by arranging it in outline form?

4

Analysis

❦ *Beer off shelves* ❦

Any problem is easier to diagnose after it has been broken down
into its parts. Yet over and over people jump straight from the problem to the solution—and tumble into the crevasse between.

I have just received a long letter from a young man who seems
launched on the wrong career. He wants my help. I can do only
what he should have done—list the issues raised by his letter, list the
various courses of action under each alternative, and then tell him
to make his choice. He has not analyzed his problem.

The young Martins decide to build a week-end cabin down by the
river. They secure a piece of land, level it, and start building with
lumber ordered as they need it. They are sure to waste time, material,
and money without an analysis of their needs—(1) plan, (2) materials, (3) tools, (4) work schedule.

Analysis is the foe of vagueness and ambiguity, those arch con-
spirators against sensible problem solving. The analytical mind insists
on definiteness and completeness. One of the ways to keep a problem
before you as you work on it is to boil it down to its essentials. By
going over a problem enough times, you can so dominate it that you
can see it as a simple structure. Perhaps you shake it down to three
short questions. Perhaps you draw it in a rough diagram. Perhaps you

reduce it to an algebraic equation. Perhaps you put it in a few sentences that your wife can understand at breakfast.

The large problem of defeating the Confederates in the Civil War was advanced by dividing the South. First came control of the Mississippi by the North, and then followed Sherman's march through Georgia to the sea. The same "divide and conquer" formula applies to many kinds of problem solving.

Suppose that as a public health official you are asked to do something about the large amount of sickness peculiar to housewives. You will not start out advocating free medical care for them. You will want first an analysis of the special kinds of troubles housewives have.

According to data accumulated by the American Medical Women's Association from the women doctors of seventeen countries, foot trouble, fatigue, anxiety, and depression are the four leading complaints. Now you know the nature of your problem. Next you want an analysis of the causes of these troubles. From the same authoritative source you get the following causes: jobs outside home; lack of protective legislation; wrong shoes; wrong use of muscles, including standing too long; difficulty of satisfying husbands' preferences for food; doing too much for husband and children; lack of labor-saving devices and inefficiency of methods of doing housework.

You have cracked one big problem up into a number of manageable smaller ones. The analysis of your solution for the main problem will inevitably follow the breakdown of the troubles and causes. It may not be easy to provide some of the answers, such as labor-saving devices, relief from outside work, and legislation to control the conditions of women's work in industry and agriculture, even though you can define those answers. But you can specify how through education the other causes of housewives' troubles can be alleviated—proper type of shoes; proper use of muscles; proper balance of devotion to family; help in the housework from husband and boys as well as from girls.

Analysis is a major aspect of problem solving. Awareness of the need for analysis will not steer you to the right form of analysis. But it will put you in the right posture to attack a problem.

Suppose that you are put in charge of a group of men being sent out to clear space in a jungle with hand tools only. Let us say that your experience in clearing jungles is nil, and that your entire knowledge of the matter is confined to boyhood observations on your grandfather's farm. You will come out pretty well if you analyze your assignment in some such pattern as this: Problem: weeds, vines, saplings, small trees, large trees. Solution: weeds—scythes and sickles; vines and saplings—brush hooks; small trees—axes; large trees—two-man saws.

The analysis of a problem is a search for a logical structure that you know from experience with other problems should be there. The intelligent problem solver approaches any problem calmly because of that knowledge. Unless you have a special interest in architecture, you probably cannot name the basic ways of covering buildings. Yet if you had to find out, you would start with the assumption that there are several but not many ways. You would find what you expected. There are four basic methods—the post and lintel, the corbel or cantilever, the arch or vault, and the truss.

Analysis of a problem, correctly made, is the major part of your diagnosis. It charts the course your attack on the problem will take. If you have a position to be filled, your analysis may be as simple as listing the requirements for the position, listing the applicants and their abilities, and matching the two. In your analysis of another type of problem you might group your factors in some such manner as this: (1) factors controllable by you; (2) factors subject to control of others; (3) factors subject to chance. In farming, the first set of factors would be the crops you plant, the acreage, etc. The second set would be regulations by Washington, market prices, etc. The third would be weather, pests, diseases, etc.

A problem may not at first seem subject to a logical analysis. It may simply break down to a list of parts or items without any discernible order. Yet it is helpful even to have a numerical analysis. If, for instance, a union is demanding eleven changes in a contract, the problem immediately has an eleven-part skeleton. A second analysis, however, will probably regroup these eleven demands into a smaller number according to kind. A third analysis will separate the key demands from the rest, the easy to settle from the hard to settle.

But the analysis of a difficult problem may be much more complex. In fact, the diagnosis of any difficult problem will usually involve several kinds of analysis. Let's look further.

The proper scheme of analysis is often dictated by the circumstances of your problem. The easiest scheme to follow is the chronological. In any process, from baking a blueberry pie to building a high-fidelity phonograph, the obvious analysis follows the natural questions: "What do I do first?", "Now what do I do?", and so on.

One of the most useful forms of analysis is the easy-to-difficult, simple-to-complex form. When you have broken down a problem by degrees of difficulty, you can often go into action, save time, and gain confidence by disposing of the easy subproblems first. In the common problem of trying to make others understand something, you will find no better plan than to proceed from the simple to the complex. This procedure sometimes takes the form of starting with the concrete aspects of a subject—what the dollars-and-cents benefits of a proposal will be, for instance—and leaving to the last the abstract aspects, such as the benefit to morale. A slight variant of this basic form of analysis is from the immediate to the remote. You might divide the financial benefits of a plan into short-range profits —or losses—and long-range profits. A similar analysis based on circumstances distinguishes what you will do immediately from what you will defer.

Classification is one form of analysis that helps make science the orderly activity it is. Linnaeus, the Swedish botanist of the eighteenth century, is one of the men who have moved civilization ahead. His invention of the binominal nomenclature system of classification through genera and species—groups and subgroups—led to the satisfactory classification of millions of plants and similar data in many fields. The present international system of fingerprinting, first put forward by J. E. Purkinje in 1823, classifies millions of finger-prints under the four heads of arches, loops, whorls, and composites.

Analysis commonly follows a breakdown of the problem into the key factors involved. You probably have not had any occasion to be-come acquainted with an opaque projector. But if you were a mem-ber of a school board being asked to appropriate funds for the purchase of such a machine, you would analyze your problem under some such headings as the following: (1) function (an opaque pro-jector is a machine that projects ordinary flat material like maps, pictures, pages of books, and student themes on a screen without the use of slides or film); (2) experience of other schools; (3) reaction by teachers and students of your school; (4) cost; (5) weight and mobility; (6) location; (7) operation; (8) upkeep and service; (9) comparison with other visual aids; (10) comparison with other tech-niques of teaching.

The mention of visual aids suggests in passing the desirability of making a visual analysis of a problem when possible. By putting your first ideas and data down on 3 x 5 cards as you analyze your problem, you can throw away the irrelevant ones and rearrange the rest in what seems the logical order. Different-colored cards can contribute to your analysis. Drawings, photographs, diagrams, and scale models are common visual aids you might use more than most of us do. When a problem is physical, you will always do well to go look at the physical factors that make it up, when you can. A look at the jungle to be cleared in the problem cited might speed up and verify your analysis and save the time that would be lost if you omitted one of the items.

For a long time a manufacturer of blankets could not explain why some stores sold many more blue and green blankets than others did. By going to the stores and using his eyes, he found the answer. Incan-descent lights made cold colors look warm; fluorescent lights made them look colder. People bought warm-looking blankets. "Go and look" often saves a lot of mental effort.

You will naturally analyze controversial problems by listing the issues. In the Dunne divorce suit what are Mrs. Dunne's charges against Mr. Dunne—1,2,3,? What are Mr. Dunne's answers—1,2,3? What are Mr. Dunne's countercharges—1,2,3,4? What are Mrs. Dunne's answers—1,2,3,4?

The issues of a problem can usually be analyzed under key words. Mrs. Dunne might have a long list of grievances that could be organized under the headings of (1) physical (Mr. Dunne gave her a black eye on sundry occasions), (2) psychological (Mr. Dunne fell asleep regularly during the opera), and (3) financial (Mr. Dunne expected her to pay his club bills out of her housekeeping allowance). Social problems often can be analyzed under headings such as historical issues, economic issues, spiritual issues. Edmund Burke—if I recall correctly—analyzed the whole problem of conciliation with the American colonies under three adjectives: (1) Conciliation was just. (2) Conciliation was feasible. (3) Conciliation was expedient.

Your first analytical task is to separate the material, relevant, important, and urgent from the immaterial, irrelevant, trivial, and not urgent. Such a diagnosis might be called selection of the significant. Selection of the significant in the analysis of a problem may put the emphasis on factors that may seem to the uninitiated secondary or even nonexistent.

After the repeal of prohibition, a long-established Brooklyn brewer decided to resume operations with a fresh design on his bottles. He engaged a marketing firm to handle the problem for him. He wanted something up to date, but he thought a hearty, traditional design that the old-timers would recognize would be in order. A friend suggested putting the Brooklyn Bridge on the label. The brewer liked the idea. Brooklyn Bridge is familiar the world over, and it was opened the same year that the brewery was founded.

When the marketing firm completed its research, the brewer agreed

30

to recommendations that astonished him. In the first place, he agreed to introduce cans because a vast volume of the beer sales would be made through grocery stores. For handling, display, and freedom from the nuisance of returned bottles, the grocers preferred cans. In the second place he agreed to a label brighter and lighter in design because in the changing post-prohibition world women were going to buy the beer off shelves just as they did the other canned goods in the grocery stores, and the label would have to appeal to them. The analysis of the total problem of selling his product revealed factors the brewer had not considered at all and gave them a decisive significance in his immediate problem, designing a label.

The Gestalt theory is the doctrine of wholes. According to this theory—and many similar modern theories in all fields—physical, psychical, or social problems are not made up of elements in a plus-plus relationship. The whole is determined not only by its constituent parts but also by their interaction on one another. The problem of running a printing plant, getting a divorce, or designing a beer bottle label might be pictured like this:

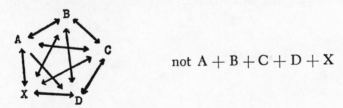

$$\text{not } A + B + C + D + X$$

If you are to analyze your problem with insight, you must see the pattern of the whole—not merely what the main parts are, but how they hang together.

Mark Pettit, trained as an artist, found himself running an advertising budget of over $1,000,000. Having no accounting or other business experience, he still kept on top of all budget problems. He did it by calling on his art training. He saw the budget as a total design, and he assigned to each part a proportion, as though he were drawing a body. At first he ignored most of the right-hand figures. He would see a major item of $253,744.16 out of a total of $1,154,889.90 as roughly a 1-to-4 proportion. He would do the same with the smaller items within the subdivisions. He weighed each item by its proportion to the whole budget and by its relation to other items.

Two simple decisions can improve your problem solving: (1) Take more time to analyze your problems. (2) Be sure the method of analysis you have selected is the most fruitful one.

• • •

Without bothering to work out an analysis of each of your past problems, review each one in your record and make a note of the method of analysis you used. . . . Make a careful analysis of each of your current problems. Are you sure that you have chosen the best means of cracking your main problem up into smaller ones? Have you uncovered all of the significant factors? Would more than one system of analysis be helpful? Can you add to the clarity of your analysis by using a graphic presentation?

5

Questions

∾ *The teddy bear or the elephant?* ∾

"THE QUESTION not asked cannot be answered," someone has observed wisely. And someone else has said, "To know what to ask is already to know half." These remarks might be put in another way: If you do not ask the right questions, you do not get the right answers. A question asked in the right way often points to its own answer. Asking questions·is the ABC of diagnosis.

Only the inquiring mind solves problems. Medical men had known for centuries that the heart pumped blood. But they had curious theories about what happened to the blood thereafter. Then William Harvey in 1628 asked the right question: Where does the blood go unless it comes back to the heart—unless it follows "a motion, as it were, in a circle?" The circulation of the blood was not difficult for Dr. Harvey to prove, once he had asked himself the right question.

The construction and application of questions is one of the principal diagnostic techniques. It is allied with all of the other techniques. The logic of the question and the significance of the words used, for instance, are matters of independent importance. But the act of attacking problems with the sharp edges of questions deserves separate emphasis.

Questions arise out of doubt. Thoughtful men who are not satisfied

33

with the solutions that satisfy others are the question raisers. The Greeks were content with the myths that explained their world so prettily. But Aristotle ended the myths by asking questions such as, "How can fossil sea shells be found in hills unless the sea once covered much of what is now land?".

In his pioneer study of business corporations, *Directors and Their Functions*, John C. Baker reports as almost the essence of his findings: "The most efficient directors are acknowledged to be those who ask the most discerning questions." Your discernment is of course limited by your knowledge of the subject. But as any lawyer or teacher can tell you, there is a special skill involved in the technique of asking the right questions and in framing them properly.

The man who made of questioning an art for getting at the truth was Socrates. He invented the question-and-answer method called dialectic. Dialectic means conversation, though you might think Socrates' conversation is rigorous. Read Plato's version of it in the *Crito*, the fascinating dialogue in which Socrates disposes of the proposal that he escape from prison and the sentence of death. You will see that Socrates is not dealing with problems that can be attacked by observation and experiment. He examines only statements of opinion. He keeps asking questions until he has reduced a statement to an absurdity or revealed it to be a contradiction of another also supposed to be true.

You do not have to add the word dialectic to your daily vocabulary. But you might with profit use the Socratic method of exploring a problem by means of an attack and defense of all positions until the false are canceled out or the differences reconciled. Your attitude, then, is one of systematic skepticism. But this method of doubting is followed in order to be able ultimately to know what to believe and in order to act. By questioning the implications of one position after another, you push on step by step through your diagnosis.

You should not blunt your use of the Socratic method by the antics of a college debate or the bullying of a criminal court. Your skepticism comes from scrupulous suspension of judgment. You raise a question for enlightenment, not to discredit. On the other hand, in raising a question, you do not espouse what may seem the inferred answer. The best way to cultivate a disinterested, unpartisan, true problem-solving attitude in other people is to cultivate it in yourself first.

Abraham Lincoln was a master at getting to the heart of a problem by means of questions. When Lincoln in his General War Order No. 1 proposed a plan for attacking the South, General McClellan proposed another. Lincoln at first rejected it, but with his incomparable willingness to suspend judgment in order to find the right solution, he permitted McClellan to put his counterproposal in writing. But he made the general toe the mark by asking the following questions:

"Does your plan involve a larger expenditure of time and money than mine?"

"Wherein is victory more certain by your plan than mine?"

"Wherein is victory more valuable by your plan than mine?"

"Would it not be less valuable in that yours would not break a great line of the enemy's communications, while mine would?"

"In case of disaster, would it not be more difficult to retreat by your plan than mine?"

Perhaps the most instructive part of this example of how Lincoln went about diagnosing his problems is that McClellan's answers convinced Lincoln to the extent of letting McClellan try his plan.

Suppose that you are thinking of opening a women's wear shop. Instead of milling around in a welter of impressions, advice, figures, and arguments, you might save time by finding answers for a series of questions like the following: (1) Who are the potential customers? (2) What is their financial status? (3) What are their basic needs? (4) What are their established buying habits? (5) What are their aspirations? (6) What variables might change their buying habits?

Your questions can control the solution of a problem. Left to his own devices, McClellan would never have met all of the issues that Lincoln raised.

The Ballantines have a long family debate about buying the lot next to their house. "What will happen if undesirable people build there?" is the question they agonize over. Finally they face the question, "Can we afford to buy the lot now?" The negative answer disposes of the problem for the present.

Your questions can also control the separate actions you take to solve your problem. Each question pushes your solution efforts in a particular direction. If you ask side-issue questions, you will spend your time on side issues. Failure to ask a key question is often the only reason for not solving a problem. Newspaper accounts of the operations of confidence men, bigamists, medical impostors, and other defrauders of the public make clear that the persons who are gulled invariably fail to ask the questions they should ask.

There is no easy system for formulating questions. Your questions follow the pattern of your thinking. You might remember that the seven interrogative pronouns are who?, when?, where?, which?, what?, how?, and why? They do not cover all the questions you can frame, but they can give you a grip on many a problem.

One way to use the question approach to problem solving is to state the essential problem as a question. There is no problem that cannot be put into a question. Lincoln reduced the problem between him and McClellan, in effect, to the question, "Which is the better plan?" A problem *is* a question. It is therefore natural to present it in that form. The direct question form has three advantages: It is a signal that you are defining the problem, not just talking about it. It has an insistent, probing quality that encourages action. And it may point in the direction the action should go.

Still, after the answer to the question, "What are the facts about this problem?", has been given, it is a good idea to ask, "What is the significance of this problem?" and "Is it a new problem?" You do not plow in with the question, "What action should we take?" First, you must ask your way to the heart of the real problem and then trace the outline of the whole of that problem.

Wendell Johnson makes two good points about questions: "There cannot be a precise answer to a vague question"; and "The terminology of the question determines the terminology of the answer."

His second point is recognized by the law. Leading questions like, "Why did you hate the man you are accused of poisoning?", do literally put words in a witness' mouth and are barred from direct examination in courts. But leading questions can legitimately lead you to the solution of your problems. The salesman who asks, "Is there anything else, madam?", cannot expect even the answer "no" to have as precise a meaning as when he asks, "Any soap flakes? soup? cereal? butter? cheese? coffee?" These precise questions first reduce the unlimited problem posed by the "anything-else?" question to manageable units. Then they bring forth meaningful responses.

Mothers know that it is often unwise to ask a small child questions that can be answered by "no," such as "Aren't you hungry?" They avoid questions that are beyond a child's ability to answer, as, "Why can't you behave like other children?" Leading questions are helpful to mother and child: "Will you have spinach or string beans?" "Do you want to take the teddy bear or the elephant to bed with you?"

You have to ask a precise question to get a precise answer. On the way out of any theater you can hear all around you the vague question, "How did you like it?" A play consists of a written text with a story, a theme, and a structure; a production with a set, costumes, and music perhaps; and a performance with actors, pantomime, diction, interpretation. The answer which this ubiquitous question brings forth is the equally vague response: "I thought it was marvelous [or I didn't like it very much]. How did you like it?"

The vagueness here lies in the pronoun "it." It has no specific antecedent. When after a performance of *Hamlet* by Maurice Evans, someone says that he thinks that "it" is marvelous, he may be expressing admiration of Shakespeare's lines without any special reference to this production. Or he may admire Evans' acting. Or he may have enjoyed a blurry sense of well-being while the play proceeded. By the time the vague pronoun "it" has been batted back and forth a few times, with a few vague adjectives like "marvelous" tied to it, the problem of giving an opinion on the play has been reduced to meaninglessness.

In business conferences, classes, and group discussions of all sorts the question that gums things up is, "What do you think of that, Owens?" Owens may have been daydreaming or may have his mind focused on a point discussed earlier. Or Owens may have missed the point of what his ears just heard. In any case Owens rarely stops to ask, "To what does the word 'that' refer?" Nor is he ever baffled by the unlimited invitation to "think." He substitutes almost anything under the sun for whatever "that" meant to the person who asked the question and starts talking. Much of the waste of time at meetings can be pinned on poor question asking.

By precise questions you can keep the discussion on the track and can also keep the pattern of thinking moving toward the solution of the problem. You can often jack up a discussion by asking: "What are we talking about now? What phase of the problem are we trying to settle?" In guiding a problem-solving conference, you can make your questions directional by reaching backward each time and summing up both (1) the idea to be commented on and (2) the position from which the comment is to be made. So you might say to Owens, "Owens, do you agree with Munsen that our training program needs overhauling?" Such a question can often so clarify what has been said and how the group is to pick it up for further discussion that Owens can say "yes," and you can pass on to other participants or to the next step. You can use a question easily, almost mechanically, to guide the discussion. "Since Owens agrees with you, Munsen, what changes would you make in the training program?"

Asking questions is like sharpening a pencil. Each apt question helps whittle the problem down to a point.

QUESTIONS

Problem solving is dealing in futures. Therefore one of the most useful of questions begins, "What will happen if . . . ?" This is the question with which the mind explores various solutions. It frees the imagination. It unleashes untried forces and forges new combinations. It is also a potent device for lining up contingencies for inspection and action if necessary. How many tragedies would be avoided if we all had a satisfactory answer for the question, "What will happen if a fire breaks out here?", or "What will we do if we have to find another source of income?" "The question not asked cannot be answered."

Why? and why not? are among the most powerful tools for problem solving that man has ever made use of. Since the dawn of civilization scientists and simple men have known that the weight of objects is related to their mass. Then Albert Einstein asked, "Why are mass and weight related?" The world-shaking theory of general relativity started with this "why?"

When you ask a question that you cannot answer, restate it. In different words it may look different. If you still cannot answer it, then, go on—ask another.

From start to finish you will find it wise to question the question. Every question makes assumptions. When an adult separates two kids who are fighting and asks, "Who started this?", he is assuming that one did. Since even small-boy fights are rarely so simple, the question is questionable. Since adult problems are more complicated, the same question may serve as an example of the kind about which you ask, "Is this a fruitful question to try to answer?" You save time when the answer is "no," and you turn to more profitable matters.

Since many problems nowadays are approached by questionnaires and tests, we might squeeze in a few remarks about them.

The first remark must be one of caution. It takes experience to compile a dependable questionnaire and experience to interpret the answers. It is nearly impossible to use words in a scientific manner.

Conclusions based on poorly framed questionnaires and tests are worthless.

You can ask three types of questions: (1) free answer, (2) two-way, (3) multiple choice.

1. Free answer—"Why are you attending this automobile show?" The person questioned answers whatever he thinks appropriate. In seeking information, you make the question directive. That is, if you really want to know about the person's reasons for attending the show, the question should not be, "Why are you here?", or "Why are you in Detroit?", but "Why are you attending this automobile show?"

2. Two-way—"Which do you prefer: automatic drive or gear shift?" The choice must be made on an either-or basis. You make the choice as specific as possible. You do not say, "Do you like the new drive or the old one?" The answerer may misunderstand what you mean by a new drive. Not caring to seem unprogressive, he may vote for the new.

3. Multiple choice—"How much did you pay for your car? [below $2500] [$2500–$3000] [above $3000]."

The free-answer type is the least exact of the three. But as a device for bringing forth opinions and facts that cannot well be anticipated, it is useful. In certain areas either-or and multiple-choice questions force choices on the person filling out the questionnaire that do not represent his exact opinion and may therefore lead you to false conclusions. Still they give you definite answers.

With experience you will find the question is like a machine tool with multiple attachments in the hands of a good mechanic. With it you can do almost everything your trade requires. With questions you can drill holes in a problem, saw it up into smaller problems, grind it down, and give the solution a smooth finish.

• • •

QUESTIONS

Read Plato's *Crito* and his account of Socrates' defense in the *Apology*. Go ahead; you'll enjoy them. . . . Mull over your record of past problems. In how many instances do you find that you failed to ask the right questions? . . . Restate your current problems in question form. What are the key questions that you are raising about your current problems? Are there some other questions where you are so sure of the answers that you are not raising the questions? Would it help to suspend judgment and ask some of these questions? Have you worded your questions as precisely as you might? Take out any vague pronouns you have used. Have you asked the questions "why?" and "why not?" often enough? Can you think of any other questions that you might ask?

6

Facts

❧ *Not enough excelsior* ❧

WE ARE all ignorant. Most of us cannot produce even a handful of accurate facts about any simple subject on which an eighth-grader should be reasonably well informed—and often is. Locate Indo-China. How is Scotland governed? What is the origin of Fourth of July? Half of the so-called information most of us carry in our heads is unusable lumber. And much of what we "know" is untrue. Someone once said to the editor-in-chief of the *Dictionary of American Biography*, "You must be one of the best informed men in America." He answered, "My mind is like a coal chute down which many tons of facts have rumbled, leaving only a little dust behind."

Diagnosis demands correct facts. You substitute observation for hearsay whenever possible. People held quaint notions about the earth they walked on until Lyell and other geologists began adding up the facts that had always been in plain sight. Fact finding is often tedious. But you cannot shirk this inescapable chore. When you learn how to mobilize your data and bring them to bear on your problems, you are no longer a rank amateur.

Because of the illness of his father, Horace, a young writer, was suddenly placed in charge of the family factory for a few months. His father's associates looked on his assignment with dismay. Yet by the end of his period of responsibility Horace had cut operation costs materially. He did it because he insisted on getting the facts straight about every situation he met. For instance, when he found two women workers having a cup of tea in the afternoon off in a remote section of the plant, he asked how they made the tea. They were using steam. An embarrassed plant engineer figured that to send the steam through miles of pipes to this point cost several dollars. And the women had been having their cup of tea every working day for years.

Much of the difficulty of problem solving comes from the impossibility of getting all the facts together before making a decision. You can also see that much trouble comes from the difficulty of putting the right meaning on the facts that you do have. Yet since you actually do not act on facts but on what you think they mean, the early stages of all problem solving require thoughtful scrutiny of the facts in hand.

A college official ruled that a certain World War II veteran was not to be admitted to college because of a poor record in high school. In plain sight was the entry after Military Record— "USNR,CY." The official saw the entry. It meant to him only that the man had been in the Navy. He did not know what "CY" meant, and he did not inquire. It meant that the boy had risen to the rate of Chief Yeoman. It meant that he had initiative, that he was able to take responsibility. And since a Chief Yeoman handles records and correspondence, it meant that there were excellent grounds for believing that he would be able to handle college work.

A fact not recognized for what it signifies has no more value than a precious stone in a savage's collection of shells and pebbles. Ignorance of the significance of facts renders us as blind to the solution of a problem as if we were matching colors in the dark. Sometimes carelessness also makes us blind, sometimes prejudice. But the well-trained person in any field, who is not ignorant, careless, or prejudiced, is still in danger of rejecting a fact because it does not fit into a scheme that he believes is sound.

Basketball coaches for many years believed that a player needed both hands to control a basketball properly. Eastern coaches went right on teaching the two-hand shot long after the superior value of the one-hand push shot had been established in the West.

The distinction between fact and opinion is obvious—when you bother to think about it. If Robinson says, "I saw a copperhead up in Mosely's pasture," you cannot say, "There are copperheads in Mosely's pasture." You can say only, "Robinson says he saw a copperhead in Mosely's pasture." What he says is a fact; what he says he saw is an opinion. If he shows you the snake and if you know a copperhead when you see one, then Robinson has reported a fact. Otherwise you are not dealing with a fact but with the credibility of Robinson in general and in the matter of snakes in particular.

Most of this book is concerned with the drawing of inferences from facts. But it is necessary to labor the point that you have to develop an acute sense of what facts are before you are in any position to reason about them. They take many shapes.

Three-year-old Harold kicks Mrs. Zwellbach's dog. This is a fact. In the quarrel that ensues the problem also involves the fact that to his mother Harold has demonstrated resoluteness of character in the face of danger. In Mrs. Zwellbach's thinking about the problem it is a fact that Harold is a cruel, undisciplined little brat who has injured a harmless animal.

Suppose that you are asked to help straighten out this quarrel. You conclude that Harold is a well-trained little boy who has defended himself bravely against an ill-trained dog. Mrs. Zwellbach, then, is doing what we all do too frequently in our problem solving. She is treating something that is not so as though it were so. She is substituting a fiction for a fact. This is the method of the wicked and the maladjusted—the cheap politician, the yellow journalist, the paranoiac, the schizophrenic. It is also the method of nice muddle-headed people, who cause more problems than wicked people do. Diagnosis nearly always includes separating fact from fiction.

One of the prime virtues of the scientific spirit is accuracy in handling facts. This effort is more difficult than it seems to have any right to be. You will find simple factual errors in an amazing number of the problems you have to solve. You will rarely get the right answer the first time when you ask for the number of anything. Business, industry, government, and the public pay billions of dollars yearly because of errors—someone bores a hole $\frac{1}{64}$" too small; someone fails to send the proper forms; someone does not use enough excelsior in packing a box; someone says there are too many engineers; someone says victory over Japan will cost a million casualties.

Counting and measurement are at the heart of scientific methods. "If you can measure that of which you speak, and can express it by a number, you know something of your subject; but if you cannot measure it, your knowledge is meager and unsatisfactory," said Lord Kelvin, the mathematician, physicist, and inventor. Lord Kelvin would be amazed, if he were alive today, to learn with what accuracy he could measure and compute with the electronic devices that would be at his disposal. Yet the scientists of today warn that accuracy of measurement is relative. A meter, for instance, is precisely and only the length between two marks on a platinum-iridium bar kept in melting ice at a temperature of 32°F. in the International Bureau of Standards at Sèvres, France.

The precision with which you can measure quantities does not apply to qualities. Unfortunately, your more difficult problems are seldom limited to measurable amounts of weight, space, or time. You can give a milling-machine operator a machine that will mill a surface to a tolerance of $\frac{1}{10,000}$ of an inch. You can give him a micrometer that will tell him what precision he has achieved. You can use a stop watch to measure to a tenth of a second the time he takes for each motion he makes. You can compute to a penny the cost of each unit he mills. But you have no instruments that will measure how interested he is in what he is doing, how much effort he will make to do what he has been taught, what his attitude toward you is, how

45

well he understands the economics of his activities, or many another matter related to his over-all efficiency.

No lesson in problem diagnosis is more important than the acceptance of the fact that it is difficult to say when you are dealing with a fact. Unless you start with the assumption that all the facts in your problem may not be as alleged, you will end with the cynical assumption that most people are liars or incompetents. If you check and double check your facts as carefully as you expect your dentist to check your teeth, you may keep your affairs in sound condition.

How do you check facts? There are three ways: (1) Whenever possible, you watch how they are assembled. If you see someone measuring a window sash from the inside with a yardstick, you have good reason to doubt his figures for the windowpane. (2) Whenever possible, you review or test the procedure used for assembling the facts. In this simple example you have the window measured from the outside. (3) When you cannot check your facts directly, you can at least question the source.

The method of securing what are called facts requires close scrutiny. When a radio commercial states, "Statistics prove nine out of ten snuff lovers use Sad Sack brand," you can be skeptical about how the figures were gathered. If each snuff lover interviewed was given a year's supply of Sad Sack, it is doubtless true that nine out of ten of those interviewed are using that brand. A wit says that some people use statistics as a drunk uses a lamppost—more for suppor than for illumination.

Here is an example that shows how the source of facts may seriously affect subsequent calculations.

The Midstate Transport Corporation planned a financial reorganization that required a fresh evaluation of its extensive holdings. The company retained Professor Dana, a leading economist, to make the complex estimate. After eighteen months he submitted his report. The reputation of the economist and the fate of the whole project were put in jeopardy when the financial vice-president, Adam Kohler, insisted stubbornly that one of the crucial final figures was too high. Bankers would not accept it as a basis for negotiations, he said. Then, since Adam Kohler had an unusual awareness of the processes of problem solving, he studied Dana's detailed report for several days. Finally a bell rang. Among the raw data that Kohler's accountants had provided Dana were certain borderline items that might have been excluded. When these were eliminated, Dana's revised report was acceptable, and the reorganization went ahead. The facts Dana first used were all accurate, and his reasoning about them was sound. But the accountants' decision about what facts were relevant included an important variable that might have caused the best solution to be rejected.

The possibility of success in solving a problem may be increased by consulting an expert. Adam Kohler had induced the Midstate Transport Corporation to retain Professor Dana as a consultant because he had sources of information and technical training in analyzing data not available to the nonprofessional. And as a leader in a group of professionals Dana had a deeper understanding of the problems in his field than the average economist. On the other hand, sometimes the guess of a person who has dealt intensively with a problem is better than the careful calculations of an expert who has not.

Nevertheless, when someone uses an expert's "facts" as part of a problem solution, be cautious. Be skeptical of assertions of fact that start, "J. Irving Allerdyce, the tax expert, says . . ." There are at least ten ways in which these facts may not be valid. (1) Allerdyce may not have made the statement at all. (2) He may have made an error. (3) He may be misquoted. (4) He may have been quoted only in part. (5) What he said may have applied to a different context. (6) He may have been joking or ironical. (7) He may have been exaggerating. (8) What he said may be generally true but not true in this exceptional situation. (9) He may not be a tax expert at all. (10) He may not be an authority in this phase of taxation.

THE ART OF PROBLEM SOLVING

Whenever someone starts quoting authorities to you—or you to them—you might remember the words of Chief Justice Charles Evans Hughes: "To whatever domain of intellectual activity you may address your inquiry, you will find in the upper levels of research and judgment grave differences of opinion among the elect few." Or you might quote the words from Sportin' Life's song in *Porgy and Bess*— "It ain't necessarily so!"

The necessity for getting facts straight leads the professional problem solver to take what seems to the layman fantastic pains in checking even small details. We can take an example from that great exercise in problem solving, the Normandy invasion. The Allies had discovered a stream that might have left a deposit of silt under the sand and shingle of the beach. Trucks and guns might bog down and foul up the invasion. One night a British naval lieutenant took a submarine through the German minefields off the coast and then paddled ashore in a rubber boat under the muzzles of the German guns. He drilled a core deep enough into the beach and brought back a thick glass tube of sand. He risked his life to check one fact: there was no silt in that spot on Omaha beach.

Mobilizing relevant and accurate data needed to solve a difficult problem often involves a good deal of reading. So much information is available in books, magazines, and newspapers that knowing your way around a library is a valuable part of your training as a problem solver. With experience you learn to grade the reliability of various sources and to check one authority against another. Men of action frequently limit their scope and effectiveness by solving their problems too largely on the basis of their own experience and that of the people they talk to. Reading provides you with facts that otherwise would never be available, since in no field can you carry in your head more than a small fraction of the accumulated information— and you never can be sure that it is up to date. In addition, reading over facts related to a problem often provides you with clues to fruitful action.

FACTS

Memory plays an interesting role in problem solving. Every day lawyers win and lose cases because of the unreliability of witnesses' observations and memories. The classic example is Abe Lincoln's securing the acquittal of Duff Armstrong. By consulting an almanac he proved that a witness could not have seen Armstrong commit the acts he said he saw by moonlight because there was no moon that night.

Since memory is tricky, the solution of a problem may be only a matter of giving your memory enough time and stimulus to release the right answer. Careful searching of the memory brings out more information about any subject than you think at first you possess. When a problem arises, sometimes the initial emotional reaction of fear, embarrassment, or irritation will lock the door of your memory. Contestants on radio quiz programs miss easy questions for this reason. Standard procedure, then, is to help channel the information from the memory. You ask yourself: "What do I know about this problem?" And you keep asking yourself. You prompt your memory by writing down what it reports to you, by reading, and by talking to other people. The effort to describe a problem to another often brings to the fore facts that were not remembered earlier. Forgetting is costly.

Along with what we might call the raw facts is the fact of the interpretation habitually put on some of them by society. Sykes and Bragdon are involved in a head-on car collision. Sykes claims that Bragdon was at fault or at least was equally negligent. He argues that even though he was approaching on the left side of the road, the marks on the road show that the collision took place in the middle. If Bragdon had remained on the right and not swerved to the left, no collision would have occurred. The facts of the accident are as Sykes states. But by the law of torts it is also a fact that he put Bragdon in jeopardy and forced him to take steps to try to avoid an accident. Therefore the court held Sykes was at fault.

You would doubtless say that it is a fact that you have the right to expel a stranger from your property. But your legal right vanishes if the intruder is so sick that expulsion would endanger his life, or if a blizzard or flood or similar condition is so severe that it would do the same. One of the rights of an American worker is to offer his services to whatever employer he likes. But this is not always a fact. The Supreme Court has ruled that professional baseball players may not exercise this right.

What you call a fact may with good reason not seem a fact to the other fellow. And you have to remember that in the solution of problems you deal with the meanings you put on facts—and so does the other fellow.

• • •

Select one of your current problems. List your facts. Do you have all you need before you try to work out your solution? Can you get more? What have you done to prove the accuracy of these facts? Have you checked them by personal observation? What is it that you do not know about your problem? Have you a clear sense of the significance of the facts that you do have? Are you accepting any unproved inferences as though they are facts? Do you know how all of your facts were assembled? Can you see any reason to doubt the source and method of assembling? Can you secure anybody better qualified than you are to check your facts? Does the validity of any of your facts rest on your memory or on somebody else's? Is it possible to interpret your facts in a different way? How would that affect your solution?

7

Assumptions

The sky was up

I<small>N THE</small> big and little problems you have to solve in your lifetime, false assumptions are invariably at the core of your troubles like a worm in a bad apple.

In your diagnosis, the first thing you do after you get the facts straight is to examine your assumptions. When an attempted solution does not come out as you think it should, reexamine your assumptions. Painstakingly answer the questions: "What have I assumed to be true in this situation? Is it true? How do I know? What am I taking for granted? Can I possibly be wrong? If my assumptions are wrong, what other assumptions might be true?" Challenging what is believed to be true about a problem that has not been solved is the quickest way to find the reason why it has not been.

Until recently the victims of heart attacks were kept in bed for weeks. Doctors were sure—that is, they assumed—that lying down placed the least strain on the heart. Then some skeptics challenged this assumption. Now patients sit up. That position gives the heart more rest.

The manufacturers of a certain furnace once asked the engineering school of Columbia University to run checks on the efficiency of two of their models. One was larger than the other and sold for $200 more. But under controlled tests, the smaller and cheaper one pro-

51

duced more heat. The manufacturers had the good sense to put what they thought they knew to the test.

The errors of your assumptions are factual, logical, and social. You assume that something is so, when in fact it is not. You assume that if something is so, then something else is so, when such an inference is unjustified. And you assume that something is so because other people think it is so, when it is not. In the end these are all errors of fact; only the reasons for making the assumptions are different.

Erroneous factual assumptions, even on the part of the leading scientists of every generation, are based on faulty observations. Progress in the practical and scientific fields is a slow correction of wrong assumptions. Thurman Arnold notes, "The idea that the sun went 'down' and that the sky was 'up' was among the greatest stumbling blocks to astronomical science for centuries." Often all that is necessary to get straightened out is to accept the implication of the facts you know are true.

In 1892 the English physicist Lord Rayleigh reported to the scientific world a puzzle that had him stumped. When he prepared nitrogen by removing oxygen from the air, it was always a little bit heavier than when he prepared it by other means. Scientists knew—or thought they knew—that air was made of only oxygen and nitrogen. Lord Rayleigh's heavy nitrogen was therefore embarrassing. If you removed the oxygen from the air, you had pure nitrogen. Nitrogen from any source was nitrogen and had to weigh the same as nitrogen from any other source. The factual error in the assumption simply had to be that the nitrogen in Lord Rayleigh's careful experiments was not pure. Air had to contain some other element, hitherto unknown. Once that assumption was accepted, further experiment removed both oxygen and the nitrogen and left a new heavy gas, argon.

Hanging on to false assumptions in the face of evidence of error is perhaps the greatest of all obstacles to problem solving. Every time you make a common-sense decision, you run the risk of basing it on an illogical assumption. Let's say your son wants to be a dentist. Dr. Vincent went to Medford Dental College. He is a first-rate dentist. You decide that if your son goes to Medford Dental College, he too will be an excellent dentist. Dr. Vincent may well be an excellent dentist, and Medford an excellent dental school. But the inference that your son will become an excellent dentist if he goes to the same school as Dr. Vincent does not follow.

Trouble arising from faulty logical assumptions is so serious that we shall devote separate chapters to the use of logic as an instrument of problem solving.

Differing social assumptions rather than wrong ones provide many of the thorns that make a briary thicket of human relations. The quickest way to find out how circumscribed your own social beliefs are, how far they can be from those accepted by other people, is to read any standard book on anthropology.

In some parts of the world marriage between first cousins is taboo. In America it is not customary. But among the Tanalas of Madagascar the preferred marriage is between a boy and the daughter of his father's sister. The daughter of his father's brother is taboo. In the Western world we practice monogamy. Possession of more than one wife or husband at one time is illegal as well as improper. In other places, however, plural marriages are encouraged. In our Western culture one of the commonest causes of murder is jealousy. We assume that jealousy is natural, an "instinctive" part of "human nature." But in the Marquesan islands three men live with one woman quite amicably.

The reason, therefore, that you have many of your problems in the first place is that you assume that certain facts are good or bad, right or wrong, because of the group beliefs that you share. Your acceptance of these assumptions adds an imperative—a must—to a problem that may not be as rigid as you think. Once, for instance, you accept the assumption that a person in your occupation and with your ambitions must adopt a high standard of living, you present yourself with a host of problems. Your efforts to solve these problems may be unsatisfactory until you challenge the social assumption from which they spring.

The trouble often lies with our hidden assumptions—the ones we accept without conscious awareness of their existence. For example, suppose that your daughter has been playing the violin since she was nine. At seventeen she wishes to stop. You react adversely. How do you use your awareness of the presence of hidden assumptions to help with this problem? First you examine your own assumptions. Music is an excellent thing. But are you justified in assuming that its excellence embraces your daughter's future? Are you sure your pride in your daughter has not led you to think she plays better than she does? Are you not assuming that musical ability has a high social rating? Is not this a second-hand judgment you have borrowed from other people without question? And deep down are you not assuming that a daughter of yours *ought* to be talented and that your daughter will be letting you down if she quits?

You then set aside the negative reaction that springs from these hidden assumptions and concentrate on other aspects of the problem. How much does music mean to your daughter? How much talent does she have? And then, too, what assumptions are involved in *her* thinking? You may discover that she has a genuine love of music and an encouraging amount of ability. But she assumes that serious interest in the violin will interfere with her popularity. You do not assume that she is wrong. You help your daughter solve her problem by bringing her belief out into the open and by encouraging her to examine it objectively. Perhaps you help her even more by suppressing your own assumptions before they make it impossible to discover what your daughter's real problem is.

Over and over in this book you will see that preconceived notions, false basic assumptions, are like landslides that divert a stream from its true bed. Over and over you will see that a vast amount of your effort as a problem solver will go toward changing assumptions—your own as well as other people's.

The upshot of this repeated activity is to develop in the skilled problem solver an ingrained, automatic skepticism. He is not cynical. He simply starts with the premise that the assumptions on which any problem rests may be challenged, just as the alleged facts may be. He is particularly skeptical about obvious answers and rigid dogmas— the things that "everybody knows are true."

Everybody in the seventeenth century, including the scientists who were beginning to overthrow the superstitions of the centuries, knew that no living things inhabited drops of water. Anyone could have told Anton van Leeuwenhoek of Delft that. But he thought he would have a look through the wonderful new gadget, the microscope. And so the Delft dry goods dealer and janitor of the city hall discovered the existence of microbes.

The habit of challenging assumptions often shatters obdurate problems the way dynamite does rock. Of course, the assumptions underlying problems are often sound. Challenging them then provides a sense of assurance. If they are sound, you know you can proceed. You know then that you are on firm ground. The assurance is doubly valuable when you secure the agreement of others involved in your problem that they share your assumptions.

•   •   •

What percentage of your past problems contained erroneous assumptions—10, 25, 50, 75, 90? . . . Apply the six questions listed in the second paragraph of this chapter to each of your current problems. Which of your assumptions do you challenge? What can you do to test their reliability? Are any of your assumptions not taken for granted by other people concerned with these problems? Can you detect any hidden assumptions that you have not acknowledged? What social assumptions have you taken for granted?

Part II

ATTACK

PART II of *The Art of Problem Solving* presents seven aspects of dealing with problems after you have made your diagnosis. Call this other main phase your attack. As in the first section, you will realize that these chapters do not represent successive steps. They are separate techniques. Unlike the methods covered in previous chapters these techniques are not all present in every solution. In any problem you will look at all *Alternatives* before you decide on one course of action, and if that does not work, you will choose another. In every problem you will weigh the *Factors* and consider the *Consequences*. Few problems permit you to disregard *Time*. But the other three chapters—*Formula, Auxiliaries*, and *Restructuring*—are modes of attack that you employ when they seem appropriate.

8

Alternatives

❧ *Happy in Syracuse* ❧

"IT CAN'T be done, chief," one of the seven vice-presidents said. "We've figured it all ways. We can't take on this contract. We haven't the capacity. We'd have to build another plant."

"How much would that cost? What other contracts could we get if we had it? Won't we need another plant soon anyway?" the president asked. The seven vice-presidents looked at their papers.

"We didn't go into that," admitted the spokesman.

"Suppose you do," the president suggested.

During one of the hurricanes that sweep the North Atlantic, a group of boatmen stood helplessly on the shore of a harbor and watched their lovely sailboats and cabin cruisers drag anchor and pound to splintered wrecks on the stones of a breakwater. As his own cabin cruiser lurched toward its doom, one owner grabbed an axe and stood poised on the breakwater. As the boat quartered onto the rocks, he jumped aboard and recklessly chopped a hole in the bottom. The sea rushed in, and the cruiser sank safely in five feet of water. After the hurricane, it was raised and repaired.

What happened? All the other owners accepted one conclusion as inevitable. The anchors were not holding. The sea was far too rough for them to get to their boats and move them to safety. The boats were bound to be driven on the breakwater and dashed to pieces. All except one owner closed their minds and said in effect, "There is no alternative." The one exception accepted the inevitability of every step except the last. He saw that there was an alternative to that, and he saved a $15,000 boat.

"There is an alternative." When you are able to say that, you crack many a problem. No single form of attack cracks more. When you are faced by a problem that offers only an unpalatable solution, you do not scream. You ask, "What are the alternatives?" If you can find even one other possible solution, you have changed the problem in a fundamental way.

A brother and sister inherit a corner plot 100 feet x 100 feet. No matter which way they divide the lot, one half will be the more valuable outside corner. Is there an alternative to this unfair division? Yes. They agree to sell the piece as a whole and then divide the money evenly.

A town librarian annually warns the library board that the increase in the number of books makes the building of a new library imperative. A committee finally investigates and agrees that since the old building will hold no more books, a new one must be built at once. At this point the librarian retires, and a new one with wider experience arrives. He finds an alternative. He sees that at least a quarter of the books on the shelves are obsolete or otherwise worthless. He clears the shelves of this dead wood and saves the town the expense of a new building for several years.

A browse through the *New York Times* will yield you a sheaf of solutions by alternatives any day. Here are four examples:

Steeplejacks could not find a way to get to the top of a high water tank from which the roof had blown off. "If I cannot go up from the outside," thought Joe Curtis, "can I go up inside?" Obviously not; the tank was full of water. Joe thought that over for a while. Then he had the tank drained, got inside, built a balsam raft, and floated to the top as the tank filled again.

The police of Glen Cove, Long Island, get relief from cracking down on young hot rodders by having the Long Island Hot Rod Association meet at police headquarters and by supervising public demonstrations of hot rod cars.

Government typists had to make an X on a medical form to show whether the answer was a "yes" or "no." Since there were eight carbons, each had to be checked to make sure the X landed beside the right word. The total number of checks each day was astronomical. Then a stenographer suggested typing "yes" or "no." No checking at all was needed after that.

Inactivity is the greatest danger to the aged. Hospitals have not the equipment, time, or personnel to help old folks stay active. Aged patients often remain bedridden for the last years of their lives, although there is no medical justification for them to be. At Ullevaal Hospital in Oslo, Norway, old people are being trained by means of handrails and exercise machines to develop their muscles to perform the one hundred and fifty or two hundred acts necessary to stay active and to take care of themselves.

The alternative to going up a water tank on the outside is to go up inside.

The alternative to cracking down on young hot rodders is to befriend them and supervise their activities.

The alternative to checking every carbon to see whether or not an X is registered beside "yes" or "no" is to write "yes" or "no."

The alternative to letting old people become bedridden is to teach them how to stay active.

In 1942 and 1943 General MacArthur's staff figured it would take ten years to drive the Japanese out of the bases they had grabbed as they swept southeast across the Pacific after Pearl Harbor. At a meeting of the top brass the experts estimated that to capture Rabaul, garrisoned by 100,000 Japanese, would alone require more planes, ships, and divisions than we had—and Rabaul was only the first of a long series of powerful bases on the road to Japan.

"Well," said the General nonchalantly, "let's just say that we won't take them." Then MacArthur unfolded his strategy of by-passing the Japanese strongholds, isolating them, and letting them "die on the vine" while the Allies, hitting where the enemy was weakest, island-hopped in giant leaps toward the Japanese homeland. It was a brilliant example of successful problem attack by finding an alternative to what seemed the inevitable.

Sometimes, of course, the reverse of this situation is true. Problems sometimes do have only one reasonable solution. Then the efficient thing is not to procrastinate and suffer but to act.

Garrison was the promotion man for a publishing house. He was full of plans for selling more books and magazines. Some of his ideas were original and sound. Others were fantastic. Most were expensive. The directors of the company were conservative, penny-pinching. They vetoed most of Garrison's ideas. He grew frustrated as the years went on. Finally he chose the only reasonable solution. He moved to another publisher who wanted exactly the kind of promotional skill Garrison had. Then he was happy. He should have seen several years sooner that he had no alternative.

Doing nothing is an alternative. It means either a choice of the *status quo* with the known solution of a problem or inert acceptance of whatever solution chance or other agencies might bring. When the consequences of doing nothing seem better than the probable results of doing something, then it is the better alternative. To do nothing is therefore no way to avoid making a decision. It is a choice of alternatives.

It usually takes no brilliance to choose the lesser of two evils. But recognition that your problem is set up on this simple basis can save much time. If the situation offers a true either-or choice, then all you have to do is match the advantages and disadvantages and make your decision.

The Knowltons are building a house with a library in a wing. Either a fine oak tree will have to be sacrificed in order to have the floor of the library on the level of the living room, or to avoid cutting through the roots of the tree, the Knowltons will have to elevate the library two steps above the living room. Awkward as the steps are, the Knowltons decide to take that alternative to save the beautiful oak.

But it takes keen analysis to reduce a complex situation to a simple either-or pattern. The purchase of 885,000 square miles of Louisiana territory from Napoleon in 1803 for $15,000,000 was the greatest real-estate deal in history. It is generally considered a triumph of Yankee shrewdness. But how did this problem look to Napoleon? Napoleon had got Louisiana back from Spain in October of 1800 by a secret treaty. Jefferson had openly threatened Napoleon that French exploitation of Louisiana would lead us to look on our old friend France as our enemy and to ally ourselves with the enemy of France, Great Britain. France and England were drifting toward war. When it came, Britain's superior navy would seize Louisiana, and Napoleon would get not a cent for it. When the crafty Napoleon had cut through the maze of international diplomacy and brought his simple alternatives into view—sell Louisiana or have it seized—he had no trouble deciding to sell for $15,000,000.

Problems often boil down to the simple form of a dilemma. A dilemma presents a choice of two solutions to a problem, both of which are unsatisfactory. That is why we speak of the horns of a dilemma. Then, as just indicated, the only answer is the classic choice of the lesser of two evils.

Long ago the Greeks saw in this fact the essence of human tragedy. *Antigone* by Euripides illustrates this tragic imperfection in the solution of human problems. Polynices is killed in opposing his uncle, Creon, king of Thebes. Creon decrees that he is a traitor to the state and must lie where he is without burial rites. Antigone, Polynice's sister, is therefore faced with a problem that has no satisfactory solution. The law of the gods demands that she perform the burial rites. She chooses to defy Creon and obey the gods. For disobeying the law of the state, she dies.

When you find yourself up against what seems a dilemma, your first move is to try to crack it—prove, if possible, that it is not a true dilemma. You accomplish this in two ways. You prove that one or both of the horns are not solid—that one or both of the statements are not true. Or you prove that the either-or choice is unsound—there is at least one other more satisfactory alternative.

Consider the common dilemma mentioned in the first chapter. Your company offers you a promotion, but you will have to leave Omaha and move to Syracuse. You and your family have your roots down in Omaha. You are happy there. You do not know that you will be happy in Syracuse. But if you decline the offer, you will doubtless be passed over in the future. You may even lose ground in Omaha.

If this is a true dilemma, you have to make a choice on the lesser-evil basis. But perhaps further analysis will give you good reason for believing that you will be happy in Syracuse. Then one horn is not solid. Or perhaps discussion with your company officials will provide another alternative that appeals to you—transfer to Chicago, say.

The more choices you have, the better your solution to a problem is likely to be. As you start your attack on a problem, therefore, you keep asking, not merely, "Is there another alternative?" You ask, "How many more alternatives are there?" The difference between the fair problem solver and the first-rate one shows up here. The superior problem solver is not thrown off by three or four possible solutions, even when they are good. The presence of any number of good answers does not mean that the best has yet been turned up. Standard practice for all problem solving, then, is to list *all* the possible alternatives before making a decision.

Sometimes, of course, one acceptable solution is as good as another, and a search for a better one is a waste of effort. Sometimes an action on an acceptable solution is more desirable than delay to secure a much better one. Perfectionists make poor decision makers when their judgment of alternatives does not embrace these distinctions.

Figuring out alternatives and making choices among alternatives is a big part of all problem solving.

Two things you should remember:

1. Choosing among alternatives often demands courage and moral judgment as well as intelligence.

2. One alternative you should always consider—*you may be wrong.*

●　　●　　●

Pick a problem that you are having difficulty in solving. List the alternatives that you have considered. Find one more reasonable alternative. List as many more as you can, even though they may not seem practicable. Is one of these possibilities worth further consideration? . . . Are you facing any problem where by doing nothing you have chosen the *status quo* as an alternative? Do you have the alternative of taking limited action? Of varying the sequence of steps in the solution? Would either of these alternatives be worth trying in place of the *status quo*? . . . In any current problem are you hung up on the horns of a dilemma? Is it a true dilemma? Are you sure? If it is, which is the lesser-evil course?

9

Factors

◈◈◈ *Favors for the ladies* ◈◈◈

AFTER the Allied breakthrough that followed the Normandy landing, General Eisenhower faced this grim dilemma: Winter was approaching. Should he dig in his fifty-four divisions across a five-hundred-mile front and wait for spring and fresh divisions and greater resources? Or should he launch a November offensive with the troops he had and hope for adequate logistic support?

If the Allies waited until spring, the enemy would build up its strength. By spring the enemy would have new jet fighters in production. By spring the enemy might discover the secret of the proximity fuse. Either jet fighters or the proximity fuse could knock our bombers out of the sky. If we waited on the western front for spring, the hard-pressed Russians on the eastern front would be bitter.

On the other hand, the Allied strength on the ground did not have the absolute superiority it should have for a winter offensive. The Germans had thirty-two divisions to our fifty-four, and they were in their own land behind the supposedly impregnable Siegfried Line. The Allied troops were battle weary. Reserves were scanty and inexperienced. Because of the enormous transportation difficulties, ammunition was so scarce it was being rationed.

Here was a true either-or dilemma with both horns cruelly sharp. Both alternatives held disastrous possibilities. The decision had to be made on the basis of weighing all factors—and they were shot full of uncertainties. Any G.I. could see the alternatives. Many officers could see the main factors. Only the Supreme Commander could weigh all the factors in the problem until the decision tilted in one direction.

General Eisenhower decided against delay and launched his November offensive. Our armies suffered greatly. But they won. Had the General made an unsound estimate of even one of the factors involved, the offensive might have been a failure. Had he weighed the factors differently and decided to wait, victory might have been long delayed.

The attack on every difficult problem involves the weighing of factors. One of the chief differences between the brilliant problem solver and the mediocre one is the exactness with which he assigns weights to the various factors of a complex problem. The chamber of commerce of a southern city decides to launch a drive by having a huge dinner with a national figure as the principal speaker. A committee works heroically for two months. Publicity, hotel arrangements, decorations, cocktails, a special menu, favors for the ladies, cigars, after-dinner brandy—every detail is figured out in advance. Well, not every one.

When the illustrious—and expensive—speaker delivers his final call to action, yawns greet his eloquence. What the committee—and many another like this one—forgot to do was to weigh the several factors at banquets that work against the success of a speaker. These are the stupefying effects of alcohol, heavy food, tobacco smoke, and bad air. Had they given due weight to each of these negative items, they would have taken steps to offset them in advance. The same speech would have been a success if it had fallen on the ears of people who had not had much alcohol, who had eaten a well-balanced meal, and who were supplied with enough oxygen.

Suppose you are going to buy a house. You and your wife narrow the field to three possibilities—A,B, and C. Your problem is to make the wisest choice. "I love the ranch type with the picture window," says your wife. "The red brick won't need painting," you say. But the third is a marvelous buy at the price, you both agree. You sit down and draw up a list of factors that must be considered: location, price, resale value, comfort, size, design, age, construction, grounds, care, neighbors, heating, and perhaps some more. You might then rate the three houses (A,B, and C) in a 1-2-3 order—location (BAC) —price (CBA)—resale value (ABC), etc. But this analysis and this rating will not give you the best answer. You have to weigh your factors. You have to decide what the relative importance of each factor is.

Now you look over your list and decide that on a scale of 10 price is the top consideration. Count that 10. Location is important, but in relation to price you rate it 7. If you are in a business that may require you to move to another city at short notice, you may rate resale value as high as location. In such a scale your wife's passion for picture windows and your thrifty notions about paint will probably carry less weight. But now if you have also worked out your 1-2-3 ratings, with the aid of a little arithmetic you can arrive at something like a scientific answer as to what ought to be your choice. Of course, if your wife still loves that ranch type with the picture window, perhaps you had better forget the arithmetic.

An editorial writer dealing with a crucial national issue, a brain specialist deciding whether or not to perform an operation, or—to use an example parallel to the one above—a real-estate broker putting a price on a house would weigh the factors, though not literally on a numerical scale. But an economist forecasting farm prices, an actuary setting insurance rates, a defense department official determining army quotas—all persons who use statistics—do assign figures when they weigh factors.

As you weigh the factors in a problem, you keep a sharp lookout for one or more *decisive* factors. Let us go back to that house you were going to buy. Suppose now we add to the problem this factor— the location must be within walking distance of a school for your two young children. Suppose further that only one of the three final choices meets this requirement. This one item dominates the decision. This, then, is the decisive factor. If in the same situation two of the houses were near a school but only one had enough bedrooms, you would have two decisive factors.

The importance of finding the decisive factors, if any, in a problem is obvious. Unless they can be worked out satisfactorily, consideration of other factors is a waste of time.

Thus your hope of a successful swift attack on a problem rests on your search for a decisive factor. It is like prospecting for uranium—strike it right, and your troubles are over. Find a decisive factor, one overriding consideration in a problem, and you may control the solution. The problem of detecting epileptics was solved when it was discovered that true epileptics are not startled by sudden noises. Why, is not known. If the people of the Near East would get rid of their ubiquitous goats, it is said, the hardships of millions of people would be alleviated. The goats eat everything green before it has a chance to grow. Thus to an extent they control the situation. But as we shall see in the chapter on cause and effect, one of the great problem makers is the assumption that a certain factor is decisive—that it controls a situation—when it does not. For instance, in spite of contrary evidence, do not most of us believe that money is a decisive factor in happiness?

Only in certain simple problems—the cost of building a house, for example, where factors (costs of labor and materials) are determinable—can you weigh the factors with sureness. Buying a house or deciding on a military offensive has no such firm system of weighing that you can look up in a handbook.

Selecting and weighing all the factors in a problem is one main technique for solving it. You seize on decisive factors, and you weigh all the factors to determine what course of action has the highest probability of success. In addition, in many problems you must of course weigh your factors according to their strength and weakness.

An accurate estimate of weaknesses will then lead you to take measures to strengthen these points.

In fact, sometimes your imaginative attack on a problem lies in building on a weakness. Many a champion athlete has been a physically handicapped boy. Many a creative artist has been a child without toys. Various sections of New England and New York that have gone down in farming, lumbering, or other occupations have come back to moderate prosperity because the impoverished land is satisfactory for chicken and turkey farms, and it is cheap. The lack of skilled workers was long a drawback to industry in the South. Recently the South has had an enormous industrial growth, for new automatic machinery has made an ample supply of unskilled workers an asset.

Your knowledge of your own affairs should enable you to determine with fair objectivity the relative importance of the factors involved in the purchase of a house. But on less familiar grounds—say, relations between the United States and Franco's Spain—the weights assigned will no doubt be highly subjective. According to the sociologist Graham Wallas, most men's decisions in political problems are the result "not of reasoning tested by experience, but of unconscious or half-conscious inference fixed by habit." And yet, no matter how unconsciously or irrationally you do it, you never escape assigning to every factor in a problem an estimate of its importance in the determination of the outcome. If you fail to include one or two factors, you are assigning them zero importance.

The aim of this chapter is to encourage you to make three efforts: (1) to spot all the factors in a problem; (2) to estimate as accurately as possible what each one weighs in relation to the others; (3) to determine whether or not any are decisive.

•   •   •

Select one of your problems in which there are a number of factors. Make a list of them. Now try out the ABC—1-to-10 system of rating the factors. The letters represent the different possible solutions; the numbers represent the weight you assign to each factor on a scale of ten. Now add up your score and compare the results with your original ideas. . . . Is there a decisive factor on your rating sheet? If there is, what is the consequence of its presence?

10

Consequences

❧ *Took back their hand-painted ties* ❧

YOU MAY recall your chagrin at the age of eleven, when your father let you jump one of his kings in checkers and then took all of your men. Sometimes you will find solving problems like that—solving one produces another. Take two of the greatest scientific advances of our age—labor-saving machines and wonder drugs like insulin, sulfa, and penicillin. The machines have made work easier and have given us more leisure. The drugs have prolonged our lives by many years. Now America has millions of elderly people without occupations.

Consider the consequences when you are examining the attack on a problem. Every action has consequences. They are part of the total problem. Some of these consequences are like the corollaries in geometry—they follow automatically. Others involve degrees of probability from certain to remote. Sometimes probable consequences of a course of action are clear to anyone. Sometimes they are clear only to the wise and imaginative.

Consider the loss-gain factors for each possible solution. Count the pluses as well as the minuses. People sometimes boggle over making decisions when the answer to the question, "What do I have to lose?" is "Nothing."

Consideration of consequences involves weighing costs of different kinds. Cost in terms of direct money payments is usually clear enough. But cost in terms of money indirectly spent, in amount of work, and in digression from other duties must be weighed. If the new telephone pole in front of Mrs. Claridge's house on Courthouse Street offends the dear lady, why not move it? According to a telephone company executive, moving one telephone pole may require 10,000 decisions by one hundred men in fifteen places. These decisions involve social, moral, legal, economic, and physical factors. "Is it worth it?" must be asked about any proposed solution.

The U. S. Army has a standard house for officers at some of its permanent posts. Presumably this design was chosen after much research and hours of discussion at all levels. It is a fine brick affair. The garage is in the basement. This ingenious feature theoretically makes the house compact, economical, and convenient. But when the house is built on flat ground, access to the garage is by means of a 45° cement incline. Heavy rains flood the garage. Snow piles at the bottom of the incline and cannot be shoveled out except by superhuman effort. When ice coats the incline, no one can back up it. Women fear to do so at any time. Result: In northern climates few of these garages are ever used. Cars stand out in all weathers or are put in separate garages built at additional expense to the taxpayer. Someone forgot to consider some obvious consequences.

Solution of one problem often gives rise to fresh problems. Slum clearance for the erection of new housing projects is fine, but frequently it has unwanted consequences. The new housing may not offer the number of units it displaces. The new rents are generally higher than the old ones. The poor cannot pay them. The result may be more crowding in other slums, dislocation of families, undesirable social change.

Sometimes a few minutes' thought shows up glaringly unsatisfactory consequences. Here is a recent table model of a famous make of radio. The talents of high-priced industrial designers were lavished on it. Instead of having dials close together on the front in the usual style, it has the volume dial on the left end of the cabinet (and inset, so that it is hard to twist) and the station dial on the right end. Preoccupation with looks, therefore, has led to the result that you have to use both hands to operate this radio—and then with much inconvenience.

We applaud the great technological advances of America. They make it possible for us to build automobiles capable of high speeds and highways on which those speeds can be maintained. Our own creative genius, therefore, is responsible for the secondary consequences—three hundred or more deaths every holiday weekend.

The United Nations sent a medical mission to the Near East a few years ago. It demonstrated that modern sanitary and medical techniques could tremendously reduce the terrible infant mortality that has afflicted the region for centuries. "But," said one of the native leaders, "what shall we do then? We are already overpopulated. If all these children live, we shall have to have more land. And the only way to get it is to go to war with our neighbors."

Of course, the consequences of an action are not always as assumed. The imaginative problem solver can sometimes foresee that the consequences of his attack will be better than other people think. Here is where figuring out the *secondary consequences*, as in checkers, is an art.

After Christmas every department store suffers a big drop in business. The usual January sales do not solve this problem. At this time of low morale in the trade, the exchange of Christmas presents adds insult to injury. The last thing a department store owner would think of doing would be to encourage the return of Christmas presents. Yet a chain of stores in North Carolina did just that. Advertisements assured the stores' customers that they would receive the same courteous service in returning a Christmas gift that they would receive at any other time. The first consequences were precisely as predicted. The ads did increase the number of people who took back their hand-painted ties and white-elephant chinaware. But the secondary consequence was a fat increase in good will and sales.

CONSEQUENCES

When you ask yourself what the actual consequences of a course of action will be, you ask, "To what degree will the obvious consequences occur?" The obvious happens more often than not. Otherwise it would not seem obvious. But the degree to which it occurs often makes the difference between accepting and rejecting a good solution. Here is an example.

A small company offering a family service in a Pennsylvania city faced the problem of absorbing higher costs of supplies or raising the unit charge for its services. "If we raise our prices again," the sales manager warned, "we'll price ourselves right out of the market. We're not selling a necessity. People will squawk and cancel the service." As it turned out, he was partly right. The company raised its charge. The customers did complain, and some cancellations occurred. But other rising prices and rising wages were changing the background of their thinking. In the main people went right on taking the service that they had become used to, and the increased income kept the company operating as it should. The sales manager calculated the result of the increase correctly in a gross sense. His error lay in measuring the degree of correctness in his calculation.

Measuring consequences must always involve the question, "How costly will failure be?" And again we distinguish in degree between total failure and partial failure. At Teheran when Stalin was pressing for an early cross-Channel invasion of Europe, General George Marshall said, "The difference between a river crossing, however wide, and a landing from the ocean is that the failure of a river crossing is a reverse, while the failure of a landing operation is a catastrophe."

One of the solaces of history is that failure to solve certain problems has sometimes been overshadowed by unanticipated benefits from the effort. The Christian knights from western Europe in the eight Crusades of the Middle Ages spent vast fortunes and countless lives trying to take the Holy Land away from the Mohammedans. They failed. But they brought back new concepts of geography,

75

trade, mathematics, science, language, and culture of immense value to the advance of western civilization. And every child knows that Christopher Columbus failed to cut the sailing time between Spain and India, but gained a new world.

Consequences must be measured in terms of ideas as well as practical effects. Thus, acceptance of Galileo's simple experiment with a ball rolling down inclines led to Newton's first law of motion on which the whole science of mechanics is founded. When Gutenberg figured out how to get multiple impressions from movable type, he did infinitely more than invent the printing press.

Effect on morale is one of the consequences of some actions. It is a key factor in executive decisions. The treasurer may be right about there being no real need to increase the mileage allowance of the sales force, but the lift to morale may outweigh the lift in cost of operation.

One of the chief reasons why executives suffer from tension is that they see the social consequences of what happens—and threatens to happen—day by day. To most members of any sizable organization the budget is about as mythical a creation as a phoenix or a wyvern. The solicitude of the officers of a firm for its budget often strikes the rank and file as fanciful, if not hypocritical. But the top men are not worrying about a budget. They are worrying about all of the men and women and children whose welfare is tied up in the figures in that budget.

Government of all kinds—the government of families and of business as well as of nations—is a compromise between freedom and restraint, between the good of the individual and the good of the group. The consequences of actions must be judged in relation to the group as a whole and to individuals and groups within the main group. The public welfare cannot be ignored even when it seems not directly or legally involved.

Through this discussion we have been looking at consequences in a passive way. We have been thinking of guarding against bad consequences. But S—the solution—equals desirable consequences. How do you know when you have the most desirable solution to a problem? Here is an illustration of the adage that the question not asked cannot be answered. If you do not raise the question, you may settle for a solution that works but is far from the best.

Setting up criteria—the means of testing the solution of a problem —therefore becomes a part of the problem attack. If you are trying to cross an unbridged stream and you find a spot where you can see that you can jump from stone to stone, the solution obviously needs no testing beyond the accomplishment. In a rough-and-ready way your criterion of the success of any solution may be whether or not it works. But many situations demand a more exact evaluation of results, often on a basis of comparison with other solutions. In certain problems, as sickness, the criterion is, how often does one solution produce satisfactory results? how often does another? In your everyday problems, however, you can generally think of your check system as $\frac{R}{C}$ —the ratio of results to cost. The cost involves money, time, effort, inconvenience. The results involve effectiveness and personal satisfaction.

The Ashlands have just completed waterproofing their large basement. It leaked so badly during heavy rains that it was used only for storage, and since it was always damp it was not good for that. The job of applying a coat of waterproofed cement to the outside and the inside of the foundations and placing a tile drain at the base of the outer wall has been a nightmare. The yard has been torn up for over two months. Mistakes have led to delays and extra expense. Heavy rains and a heat wave have made working in the sticky clay disagreeable. Labor and materials have cost more than seemed possible. The inconvenience to the Ashland family has been enormous. But so far it seems likely that the job will be effective. The Ashlands will not know for a few years whether or not they can count on permanency of results. And they have no evidence that their method is better than any other. If someone proves that a basement under heavy water pressure can be waterproofed from inside, then the Ashlands clearly missed the best solution. But if they get a dry basement that can safely be divided into a storeroom, an extra bathroom, and a workshop, they will agree that the quotient of $\frac{R}{C}$ will be satisfactory.

Consideration of consequences, secondary as well as direct, is a big part of problem solving. Setting up criteria to test results is an inseparable part of your job. Sometimes your success is easily demonstrated. Sometimes, as in science, it can be demonstrated only by elaborate technical proof. Sometimes, as in art and human relations, it can be judged by opinion only. Yet you have not thought out your attack on a problem until you have estimated what the consequences of each effort to solve it will be.

•   •   •

Reconstruct the steps you took in working out a past problem that has not turned out successfully. Can you see where you estimated the consequences of your actions incorrectly? Do you have any examples where your solutions of problems created worse new problems? Any examples where the secondary consequences outweighed the primary in value? . . . Now turn to a present problem that you are about to take action on. Make a list of all of the steps you will take in carrying out your attack. Now list the consequences of each step as definitely as you can. Does this review lead to any modifications in your plans? Keep the list and check your estimates against the actual results. . . . Go back to the list you just made. Can you distinguish between tangible and intangible consequences? Write out your criteria for testing the success of your solution. Check these criteria later when you check your list of consequences.

11

Time

❧ *"Risky to spit on one's hands"* ❧

THE late Hiram Rivitz, founder of the Industrial Rayon Corporation, once received a long-distance call from a young business associate. The young man said: "I'm going to buy a textile mill in Memphis for $200,000. The government is letting out some fat contracts very soon. What do you think?" Rivitz replied: "You say you're going to buy the mill, and *then* you're going to get a contract. That's your business, son, but I'd get a contract first. Then I'd know whether I had any use for a mill."

Napoleon said: "At Montebello I ordered Kellermann to attack with eight hundred horse, and with these he separated the six thousand Hungarian grenadiers before the very eyes of the Austrian cavalry. This cavalry was half a league off and required a quarter of an hour to arrive on the field of action. I have observed that it is always this quarter of an hour that decides the fate of a battle."

Time is a factor in your attack on most problems. Have you ever stopped to think what miracle of time management the erection of a high office building in a city is? Where does it start? With men thinking, talking, planning. The financing that must precede the construction is made by men who must take risks on the basis of their estimate of business conditions several years hence. Long before the excavation begins, an agent is renting space, and tenants are

79

terminating leases elsewhere. Orders for steel have been placed, and there has begun the elaborate time schedule of turning the iron ore from the Mesabi into steel girders with holes punched exactly where months later a riveter will insert a rivet. No small part of the miracle is the fact that the busy traffic of the city must continue to swirl about the site of the building. Girders and plumbing supplies and cement and electrical equipment and tiles and glass and every single item must arrive and be received without blocking traffic. That means that deliveries from widely separated points, from many different firms, must be staggered and coordinated to arrive so that they will be available the day that they are needed. The dollar losses on delayed deliveries can be great. Through all of this enormous cooperative effort men and women are at war with time. And the typist and the truck driver, the draftsman and the accountant, as well as the executives, have a role to play.

Time is as decisive in many of your problems as it was in Napoleon's. It is so critical and it is so commonly overlooked that you should add to your analysis of every problem the query: "What about T, the time factor?" Most important: "When must the problem be solved?" Raising $500 in cash may not be a difficult problem. But you might find it far from easy on a Sunday afternoon.

The solution that is not ready in time is not a solution. The solution that is presented at the wrong time may sometimes as well not be presented. A sense of time and of timing is part of your equipment as a problem solver. Your effectiveness includes your ability to foresee clearly what T, the time factor, equals in the equations you set up, not only for yourself but for others. You cannot give yourself a good rating if you drop a folder of copy on someone's desk with the remark: "Will you check the figures in this stuff, Milton? By the way, the printer is sending a messenger for it in half an hour."

As a person with responsibilities you live as much in the future as in the present. The heavier your responsibilities, the more the future concerns you. Young men and women go through four years of col-

80

lege and often more years of graduate school without acquiring much time sense at all—perhaps because their professors have time measured for them by the ringing of bells. Education should help men and women to understand how implacably the problems of the working world are bracketed in time.

Take a simple example. Tim Halloran has his first job as supervisor of athletics in the schools of his home town. Tim gets notice to submit his budget estimate by a certain date. He looks up the carbon of his predecessor's requests and asks for the same amounts. Then he forgets the budget. Several weeks later Tim has a fine idea. The school playgrounds could be resurfaced and marked with permanent lines. Then the boys and girls could play tennis, volley ball, basketball, and other games out of doors much of the school year. This device would relieve the crowding in the inadequate school gyms and get the students out in the fresh air.

"The idea sounds interesting, Tim, but the money isn't in the budget," says the school superintendent. "You submitted your requests some time ago. The Finance Committee completed the whole school-system budget weeks ago. The Board of Education has approved it. Now the Budget Director has it. He and the Mayor are working on it. Next month it will go to the City Council. . . . Let's talk about your plan next year, Tim."

A few weeks later Tim is back with a plan for having the city sponsor the state relays that May. And once more he has to be told that since there are no funds for such an activity in the present budget, and since he did not make a request at the proper time for inclusion in next year's budget, once more he is talking about something that cannot happen until the year after next.

To find time is one of your most insistent problems. You may ponder the wisdom in the whimsy of Bernard Berenson, the noted scholar of Renaissance art, who at eighty-six, to secure the time he found so precious, said, "I think I shall stand at a corner hat in hand and beg passersby to drop in their wasted hours." You are the caretaker of your own hours. If you do not have time to solve the problems that press you, then you are neglecting your number one problem. The solution may range anywhere from the simple procedure of organizing your activities and following a written time schedule, all the way to changing your life pattern so that you are doing what you consider most important instead of putting it off until some day in the dim future.

The time at which you solve a problem may make the difference between success and failure. For instance, Kurt Lewin points out, adopted children who do not learn until the age of seventeen or so that they are "only foster children" and they "don't belong" often suffer a severe shock in spite of being surrounded by affection. Now placement authorities advise foster parents to tell children the truth early and to emphasize that they are especially "chosen" children. The same solution but a different T-factor.

With the passing of time problems change. This platitude is often overlooked. When you take a new job, often you will hear: "Oh, that won't work. We tried that." You can point out—to yourself—that you are new, and you therefore change the problem by providing a new element. Every day you will hear people talking about a changing situation as though it were static. It is, for instance, nonsense to talk about marital differences, labor relations, or foreign policy as though they were made of iron—like the deer that used to stand out on the lawns of the gentry in Grover Cleveland's day. In human relations the forces that create problems rearrange themselves constantly like the clouds, and the problem of today may well be as different from the problem of yesterday as today's sky is.

At twenty Marty Gates is sure that the main problem of his existence is to be together with Linda Sanderson always. At thirty he sets a partnership in his firm as the target of his endeavors. At forty he seems to be working for the house he and Linda have built and to pay for the cost of bringing up a family according to the American standard of living. At fifty he looks forward to retirement—to escape from the struggle or to the attainment of a deeper philosophy.

You often have to count on time lag. Many of the problems that you try to solve are splinters of larger problems. You may feel frustrated because you can see clear solutions, and you cannot understand why society has not adopted the large one long since so that you can carry out the smaller one. But you learn to take the T-factor of time lag into account. As you deal with problems over an extended time, you will watch for a tendency, and you will abet or counteract that tendency very much as a helmsman eases or checks the headway of a sailing vessel by tiller and sheet.

Men talked for years about the possibility of linking the Great Lakes and the Hudson river to provide a waterway between the Middle West and New York and the sea. The technical difficulties were not a major hindrance. But the Erie Canal did not become a reality until exploration of the West, gift of western lands to the veterans of the Revolution, and crowding on the seaboard shaped the action. The St. Lawrence Seaway has had much the same history. After fifty years, international tensions have finally brought about its beginning.

Your attack includes calculating the timing of your moves while you are solving a problem. You will often commit yourself to one step at a time in going the whole distance that you plan to go. For instance, having planned a number of improvements in your house, you might carry them out on a schedule according to your ability to pay for them.

Two enterprising young men who had started the *Star*, a newspaper in competition with the long-established, well-financed *Journal*, were faced by a critical problem when the price of newsprint jumped several times in as many weeks. If they did not increase the price of the *Star* to the readers, they would soon be losing money and have to quit. If they raised the price of the *Star* right then, the wealthy owners of the *Journal* might hold out and take their losses in order to cut down the circulation of the *Star* and drive it out of business. On the other hand, if the *Journal* raised its price first, the *Star* would run into much less resistance to an increase. Faced with this dilemma, the two young men decided to borrow money and postpone their increase on a day-by-day basis until bankruptcy was so few hours away that they had no alternative. The owners of the *Journal* misjudged the young men's staying power and raised the price of the *Journal*. The next day the *Star* raised its price and stayed in business.

Delay is not always a disadvantage. It is often an end in itself. Battles are sometimes fought for the sake of winning time. Defeats that throw off the enemy's time schedule are strategic successes. You will frequently find that your first decisive step in attacking a problem is to gain a delay. Extra time can be a plus factor in the equation.

There will be times when you must say, "This problem is temporarily unsolvable." You will then turn aside and go to work on other problems. Time will give you a chance to rest your brain. Time will give your subconscious a chance to work on the problem. Time will allow you to consult others. Perhaps you will need only the traditional "time to sleep on it." Perhaps you will need years. Problem solving is like playing football. You often have to maneuver patiently for an opening and then drive through.

Experience in problem solving should give you the kind of time sense that is sometimes miscalled patience. The solving of long-range problems does not necessarily give you that sweetness of disposition implied by the word patience. You may be impatient day after day for years. Most people who solve important problems are more determined and persevering than sweet tempered. What they have is a sense of objective so sharp that it jumps time for them. The activities of the moment are linked in time with the outcome of events months or years ahead. This sense of the immediacy of the future keeps them driving when other people are coasting along because their time sense is too limited to invest future events with urgency. Yet it is your ability to measure the distance to your objectives in terms of time that will permit you to ease up on occasion. Your awareness of degrees of urgency will tell you whether or not you should heed the advice that Secretary of War Stimson gave to President Roosevelt: "In a tug of war it is highly risky to spit on one's hands even for the purpose of getting a better grip."

The United States is so young a country that Americans have not the time sense that other peoples have. Wherever Europeans and Asiatics turn, they are surrounded by reminders that other men and women, some much wiser and many equally foolish, sought the solutions to similar problems yesterday and a thousand years ago. You will find that the perspectives you gain by reading history and biography will be among the practical aids you have in grasping your own problems and the larger problems of your times.

• • •

Examine several of your problems. How does time operate as a significant factor in them? Is it a decisive factor in any? In which ones does the passing of time change the structure of the problems? In which may old discarded solutions or fresh new ones conceivably be acceptable? . . . How are you managing your daily problem-solving time? . . . As you review the problems you are working on, how does the T-factor influence your attack? How does the timing of your various steps and of your final decision affect the success of the whole operation? Can you make your efforts easier and the outcome more satisfactory by changing your timetable in some way? . . . Make a list of your personal and professional objectives. Take each one in turn. Would it increase your happiness or your professional effectiveness if you moved those objectives nearer in time? farther away?

12

Formula

✑ *"Lady, where does this go?"* ✑

A FORMULA is like a basket. Try to pick up a dozen apples from the ground and carry them in your hands. It is well-nigh impossible. With a basket you can carry as many as you can lift.

The sergeant who selects the men for a mess detail by shouting, "Abbot, Ackroyd, and Adams!" is using a time-honored formula. When he puts Abbot, the first on the list, in charge of the detail, he uses the same formula over again.

When the Stouffer chain of restaurants was in its early days of expansion, Vernon Stouffer and his associates found the usual restaurant layout unsatisfactory. It did not suit the type of service they were creating—high-quality food at moderate prices for a large number of people. In time they arrived at a formula unique in restaurant management—the working area of the restaurant behind the scenes must equal the dining area out front. Vernon Stouffer believes that this formula has contributed much to the successful operation of the chain.

Law is a formula for solving certain of the problems of society. Within that large system are many thousands of smaller formulas— laws, that is—for handling smaller problems. Medicine is a formula for dealing with disease. Streptomycin and other drugs, rest, food, and fresh air make up a formula for treating one disease—tuberculosis.

86

FORMULA

We are surrounded by such formulas for dealing with problems. All human action is a complex of such systems. Yet we go right on trying to solve our own problems by picking up apples in our bare hands. We are chagrined when they spill back over the ground.

Most of us could increase our personal efficiency by formularizing the way we attack many problems that now we tackle hit or miss. By not having a formula, we often have to think about inconsequential matters that do not deserve thought. For instance, Jenny kept forgetting to turn off her electric stove because when it was turned low it was hard to see that the heat was on. She solved this problem by establishing a rigid habit of turning the heat off first before she allowed herself to touch the coffee pot or pan that she was picking up. Habits are formulas—some good, some bad.

One of the simplest ways to formularize many of the problems that harass most people is to write things down—make a note, make a list. Haskill sees Boggs in the lobby of his office building and discusses an urgent problem at length. Boggs makes no notes. When the problem comes up, Haskill is annoyed because he has to brief Boggs again on the details. A pocket notebook would have saved Boggs embarrassment. An office supervisor is told to get in her annual requisition for supplies by four o'clock. She rushes around asking for individual requests. People try to think. The day after the order goes in, she finds that thumbtacks, typewriter ribbons, and half a dozen other necessities were overlooked. An office-supply check list—a formula—would have solved this problem with ease.

But the formula as a technique for solving problems can be used in a more specialized way. Breaking a problem is often like opening a safe. The numbers used are simple enough. But only one combination of the numbers will do the trick.

The state of Ohio for years had trouble finding properly qualified men for the State Highway Patrol. It took the best of the men who applied, but it was not having as many good men apply as it needed to make the right sort of selection. What plan could be found to take the place of the haphazard lack of system that prevailed? Someone found a formula—a training school. Now the State Highway Patrol of Ohio takes its pick of the best of the graduates. By much the same formula business concerns that used to have acute difficulty filling top executive positions now have upgrading programs for their junior executives.

The wife of a busy manufacturer found herself coming off second best in competition with her husband's business. Instead of drifting into the standard role of the neglected wife, she worked out a formula with her husband. Every Wednesday she goes to the city for a hairdo and shopping. Then she meets her husband for dinner and the theater. Saturday they spend in the country at her brother's farm. Sunday they explore the countryside for a pleasant place to have dinner. This formula does her husband as much good as it does her.

The Gerards have had to move every year or two because of Bert's business. At first it was a nightmare. As the moving men came into the new house, Lisbeth and Bert would run around saying things like: "Oh, that chest of drawers doesn't go up here in the bedroom. It goes down in the dining room." "Sorry. That's the extra refrigerator. I'm afraid you'll have to take that down in the basement."

Then Lisbeth borrowed a formula from her backstage experience in a little theater. She drew a floor plan of the new house and indicated where each of the major pieces of furniture should go. Then she numbered each of the rooms and stuck a sign on it. On each piece of furniture she stuck a piece of masking tape with the proper room number on it. Now the movers, instead of standing in the middle of the front hall balancing a sofa on their heads and asking, "Lady, where does this go?", walk straight to the right room. Then with the master plan to guide her, Lisbeth simply points and says, "That goes there."

The civilian manager of the cafeteria in a Navy installation complained that the sailors were so slow in going through the line at noontime that he could not feed the number contracted for in the hour allotted. He asked for disciplinary treatment of the stragglers. The captain decided to have a look himself. No sailor dawdled. Still the line had not been fed at the end of the hour. "Suppose you try this," he suggested to the baffled manager. "Instead of having the men put the heavy items and the ones that are hard to carry, like milk and coffee and soup, on their trays first, shift them to last, and put the light and easy to balance things like bread and meat first." The formula put the line through inside the hour.

The captain was not a cafeteria expert. The manager was supposed to be. But the captain saw a problem. He saw it in its simplest elements—time and the factors that controlled the time it took one man to fill his tray and walk the length of the serving counter. When he saw what those factors were, it was easy for him to rearrange them in the formula that permitted the most speed.

What you do to a situation when you use the formula approach is to schematize it. You impose a pattern on it, a shape—very much as a cooky cutter does to dough. You do not, in a way, think about the dough—the stuff that your problem is made of. You think of the shape—the way it should look, the right design. You may not understand what the details of the problem are all about. Few executives can know all the technical details buried in the problems about which they make decisions. They still are able to relate different recommendations to an over-all design of purposes and operations.

Alec Streeter, an ornithologist, inherited a prosperous small leather business from a cousin. Two of the employees offered to buy it, and he agreed to sell it to them at a fair price. He did not know the true value of the business. How could he impose a formula on this problem so that he could cut out the exact amount, nice and clean? Streeter was soon besieged by brokers who offered to sell the business for him. Without committing himself to any one, from each of them he drew an estimate of the best price he could be sure to get. Then he struck an average, subtracted what would have been the broker's commission, and sold the business to the employees for what they agreed was a reasonable figure—but not the bargain they had privately hoped to get from a fellow whose business was birds.

Let us imagine that Hazel is shy and finds conversation with strangers an ordeal. How can she carry with her to a dinner party, say, a ready formula that will see her through? How can she avoid the inane formula of the weather? She can rely on the formula used by many shy people who have been forced by circumstances to do a great deal of talking to people they do not know. She simply asks the questions that cover the four topics of home, family, occupation, and hobbies. With encouragement, almost anyone will talk on any one of these topics as long as anyone else will listen. Let us say that Hazel finds herself at a dinner seated next to a novelist from Hungary. She has never read a word the man has written. Instead of silently submerging herself in her soup, she might easily get him to talk about what it was like to be a boy growing up in Hungary. And if Hazel holds to the formula she will forget her shyness as she explores the answers she gets.

Nothing about the use of a formula, of course, prevents your adding to the crude framework you start with. To use a formula does not mean to use it mechanically, without variation. You will find it useful in attacking unfamiliar problems to abstract a formula as fast as possible. But it is to be used as a point of departure, not as a rigid form. Here the symbol of the cooky cutter used earlier is not appropriate.

Rigidity is the obvious danger in the use of a formula attack. Formula-thinking cripples the problem-solving abilities of many people. Business executives and military men have a passion for drawing up organization charts and hanging them on the wall. To try to run a complex organization without a clear understanding about who does what and who answers to whom is to dally with chaos and catastrophe. To picture the chain of command in a cluster of boxes connected by lines may be a helpful formula. But it is only symbolic. It is not the reality. The reality is people. They refuse to stay within boxes. They do not in actuality run along the designated lines of communication like electric currents in a circuit. To insist on rigidity of communication is to set up a *closed system*. In a rigid-formula system when one unit stops functioning, the whole organization slows down or stops.

If your formula assures you of the right answers in advance, you are operating within a closed system. A closed system is one in which all questions are answered by being referred back to the ultimate authority of some person or dogma. Just as a company goes to seed when nobody but the boss ever has authority to make a decision, so your competence as a problem solver shrivels once you become convinced that you can find all the answers in organization charts, regulations, or "talking things over."

Business decisions may be roughly formularized as follows: Of several alternatives of apparently equal merit, choose the one that seems best to advance the objectives of the organization. Of several alternatives that seem equally to advance the objectives of the organization, choose the least expensive. The value of some such formula lies not so much in producing the right answer as in hacking through confusion and indecision—in providing a way to see what are really the advantages and disadvantages of various solutions—in speeding up the decision time.

But the use of a formula in your thinking can do more than help you get a hold on a problem. If, for instance, you are asked to investigate the management of an orphans' home, you try to relate your observations and judgments to a system of thought of some valid kind. You may know nothing at all about orphans' homes, but you might take as a reasonable formula that all children need affection and security before they need anything else, and start working from there. Reference to a system of some kind can be a valuable integrating force in your thinking.

Custom is one of the devices by which mankind uses a formula for easing the problems of living. It makes little difference in terms of survival whether you eat your dinner at noon as country people do, at six as townsmen do, at seven as suburbanites do, or later as society folk do. But eating at a certain hour is a formula to make life seem predictable. The more pattern we impose on existence, the more sense it seems to make.

The elaborate marriage customs of the upper-crust Cambodians and Chicagoans have no relevance in terms of efficiency, but they give a number of people a sense of importance doubtless good for their egos. Americans who have endeavored to increase the efficiency of the business procedures of the British, the Indians, or other tradition-directed people have rarely accomplished much. Ways of doing things that have the sanction of custom are often inefficient in an ordinary sense. But since they are understood, they reduce effort and friction and therefore have a real efficiency after all. And since they make people who do them imagine that they are living in a stable universe, they serve to solve problems larger than the limited ones they solve poorly.

Many problems are easy to solve once you apply a formula—a plan, a policy, a routine, or a system of some sort. Formulas liquidate problems. When you reduce similar recurrent problems to routine treatment, you come nearer to settling them permanently. When, in the examples previously given, Streeter invented a formula for setting a price on the leather business, he had no further use for it. But if Hazel's formula works on the Hungarian novelist, she can use it until her shyness disappears. The reason for taking pains to solve one problem properly, therefore, is that with luck the solution may be applied over and over. You have achieved what is often the true aim of problem solving. You have not merely solved a problem—you have gained control of the problem situation.

•   •   •

Think over the activities that make up your typical day. Which are formularized? How efficient are your formulas? Would it help to impose a formula on any of the others? . . . Now consider one of your urgent problems. Do you have a formula for attacking it? If you do not, can you find one? If you have one, are you using it as a means of getting hold of the problem quickly or are you using it mechanically to solve the problem? . . . Can you discover any places where your daily problem solving is handicapped by closed-system thinking? As you solve individual problems, are you turning any of your solutions into formulas for solving similar routine problems in the future?

13

Auxiliaries

❧ *"Do it with a sleight"* ❧

WHEN Roland Hayes, the famous Negro singer, was young, his first job was in a foundry. He was put with a gang loading a freight car. Eager to make good, he grabbed his wheelbarrow, wrestled it up the plank runway, and dumped the load with a mighty heave. As he returned for a second load, an old Negro stopped him. "Look, son, that no good nohow. Yo' wear yo'se'f all out. Yo' gotta learn to do it with a *sleight*." Trundling the loaded wheelbarrow easily up the runway, with a slow rhythmical twist he dumped the load. "Yo 'member now, boy. Yo' do it with a sleight."

Roland Hayes remembered all his life, through the grueling physical and emotional strain of practice, teaching, travel, rehearsals, and performances of a concert singer and teacher. He learned to take music and life "with a sleight"—not to try to handle heavy weights or problems by a dead lift but to add an extra bit of rhythm or humor or faith.

Problems that do not respond to other methods can sometimes be worked out by the use of auxiliary devices of one kind or another. You might say an *auxiliary* is a device that aids in the solution of a problem of which it is not originally a part. It is a sleight or, in slang, a gimmick.

The Fillmores rented an apartment on the top floor of a five-story

94

building. The house had no elevator. The mover found that there was no safe way to raise their grand piano outside of the building and swing it in through a window. His pocket ruler would not tell him with certainty whether or not his men could get the piano around some narrow turns in the staircase. So he had an exact mock-up of the piano made in cardboard. It would not go. This is an instance of *substitution*, the first type of auxiliary.

The oil that facilitates the turning of a nut with a wrench or the hot water and shaving cream that aid the mowing of whiskers with a razor are examples of the other main type of an auxiliary. It might be called an *additive*. In these examples the auxiliary, though not a part of the original problem, makes a definite contribution. At first the wrench does not turn the nut, and the razor pulls the whiskers. The wrench plus the oil and the razor plus hot water and shaving cream get satisfactory results.

A more ingenious variation of this second type of auxiliary is the additive that makes the solution possible without merging with it— without becoming a substantial part of it. This third kind of auxiliary might be called a *neutral* or *zero factor*.

If a body of men have to walk ten miles, the addition of the sound of a marching band playing "Washington Post March" or "Bugle Call Rag" will not enter into the physical operation of the legs, but it will aid it. In the case of extraordinary fatigue it could make the difference between reaching an objective and not reaching it. Prayer has frequently made this difference.

Now let's give these three auxiliaries another look.

The classic statement of substitution is the mathematical "Things equal to the same thing are equal to each other." How in practical affairs can you solve a problem by applying this mathematical idea of equivalents—A equals B; B equals C; therefore A equals C? Actually, outside of mathematics this state of affairs rarely exists in any such perfection. The symbols of mathematics are abstractions. If C equals

A, you can put it in the place of A because it corresponds precisely to A, as two right angles do.

You cannot expect people and things to correspond with the perfection that symbols do. But you can use the same principle of equivalence fruitfully. Perhaps the most usual equivalence of people and things is that of function—they can be used to serve the same purpose. They are not necessarily alike in any other sense. But you can substitute one for the other and so solve your problem. The use of women as machine-tool operators during wartime is an example.

Your law firm has a big case come to trial during the summer. Two of the law clerks stay on the case through August and miss most of their vacations. The pressure of work during September does not permit you to let the men extend their vacations to their full length. You therefore give them a salary bonus in lieu of the vacation time lost. The money does not equal the time, but it is a passable substitute.

In genetics and other biological sciences research on human beings is often impossible because experiments may involve death or damage to the subjects and also because the scientist cannot live long enough to see the results of his experiments on several generations. Therefore flies, mice, and other creatures that have a brief life span are used as substitutes.

Substitution of the more familiar or more normal for the less familiar or more exceptional is another variation of this technique. "Gimmick" for "auxiliary" is an example of such substitution in language.

Suzanne, an exchange student from Paris, tells the dean of women of her college that she does not care for dormitory life and would like to live in town where she might pursue her studies with less distraction. She is a mature girl with much charm, and the dean is inclined to agree. But the dean asks herself what her answer would be if instead of Suzanne an American undergraduate were to make the same request. After this substitution the dean realizes that Suzanne's personality does not change the circumstances sufficiently for her to set aside the regulations.

There is a mossy joke about a moron who found a strayed cow when everyone else had failed. "It was easy," he said. "I just thought where I'd go if I was a cow. I went there, and there I was." Imbedded in the old joke is a useful pattern of imaginative substitution. You might use it.

In the more than eighty years the Chicago stock yards have been in existence 500,000,000 hogs have been unloaded, according to Harold H. Martin in the *Saturday Evening Post*. They have been forced down cleated ramps only by means of blows, with poles, prods, electric buzzers, punches, kicks, and curses. Seeing this messy procedure for the first time, Wood Prince, new president of the Union Stock Yards, asked his general superintendent, Frank Flynn, why a hog chute in the form of a flight of stairs could not be built. An old hand, Flynn in all his days had never heard of hogs being driven down a flight of stairs. But when the first experiment was tried on a stairway adjusted to the short legs of the hogs, they tripped down happily.

Prince attributed his success in solving this centuries-old problem to his "ignorance of hogs and the historic methods of handling them." Martin adds: "If he had been an experienced livestock man, steeped in the tradition of the yards, the simple thought might never have occurred to him that if people feel more surefooted and confident on a stairway than on a sloping ramp, a hog might feel the same way."

Sometimes substitution is a matter of values. Peter Hanford puts in several years getting a Ph.D. in economics. His wife is sad because he has so little income and fun during those years. But Peter points out that he cannot fairly compare his state with that of other people who are giving the same years to making money and enjoying themselves. He hopes to have a good income and more security in the future. He is also mastering a subject that interests him more than anything else does. He has solved the problem of his career by making substitutions of factors that are equivalent in their values.

Since the ancients discovered that adding yeast to grain aided fermentation, solving problems by adding a factor not present in the original conditions has been common. In its usual form the element added merges with the other elements and becomes part of the structure. That is true of innumerable other familiar formulas, as it is of yeast—the flying buttress that permits the Gothic cathedrals to soar aloft without tumbling down, the shock absorber on a car, the additional cameras in three-dimensional movies, the adopted child in a childless family.

Recently I have been laying a brick terrace. To cement each brick into place would be tedious, messy, and expensive. Yet each brick (especially the second-hand type I am using) has to be set firm. "You bury them about two inches in sand," says one kibitzer. That seems a boring and difficult business. Then Art Blickle says: "You just lay the bricks on even sand. Then you sweep sand over the tops and into the cracks. That locks the bricks." It does. It is an inspired piece of problem solving. It is a perfect example of an auxiliary that yields a successful answer by adding a factor not given in the original statement of the problem.

It is curious how long it has taken the human race to figure out some inevitable additions. For many centuries seafarers sailed with the wind and no other way. Then some genius added a keel to his boat and sailed upwind as well as down. Civilization entered a new phase. For centuries the Monday wash dragged on the ground because clothespins worked loose. Then some genius added a spring—known from ancient times—and housewives cheered. Ever since the common woodscrew has been in use—several centuries now—carpenters and Saturday afternoon handymen have been cussing as they tried to keep a screwdriver from twisting out of the screwhead notch while they executed a full 360° turn in an awkward position. Then some genius thought of adding a notch to form a cross, and the indispensable Phillips screw was born.

If you look about, you will find plenty of problems that might be solved by adding something. The glass top on coffee percolators would not fall off with such infuriating ease if it were threaded or fixed securely instead of inserted loosely into notches in the cover. Have you ever watched moving men lifting heavy pieces of furniture onto the tailgate of a van from the ground? Either they make a dead lift, or they drag, shove, and carry things like refrigerators up slippery planks. You wonder when an electric lift will be standard equipment of moving vans to make this part of the task easier, faster, and safer. Still, this reluctance to adopt a recent invention is not remarkable when you notice how few husbands utilize the principle of leverage when their wives ask them to open a window that is stuck.

Adding an element to the ingredients of a problem to promote a solution without having it become part of the structure is somewhat trickier.

Mathematics and chemistry use this technique commonly. Chemists often add tracer elements in order to follow the course of chemical actions. Barium taken in the morning reveals in the doctor's fluoroscope how the patient is digesting his food. Isotopes injected into mice can help determine the progress of disease.

Builders use this type of auxiliary in many ways. Temporary wooden forms for concrete are one illustration. Guy wires are another. You have often seen bricklayers stand on a temporary scaffolding outside of the wall they are building. Without it they would be helpless. Now they have to put the window sashes in those walls. How do they do that? Do you think they lay the brick so accurately that they force the sashes in place exactly as they should be? Apparently that is not practicable. Then what? They cannot hold a sash in mid-air with one hand while they brick around it. Not quite. What the builders do is construct a temporary wooden frame that holds the window accurately in place while the wall around it is completed. Then the frame is removed.

Forwarding the solution of a problem by adding something that adds nothing substantial to the completed solution calls for imagination. Music and restful colors in a factory, color added to dangerous insecticides, pleasant odor added to common scouring powder, moving the clock ahead an hour for daylight saving time are examples of such additions.

In human relations emotion is the most common auxiliary of this sort. You write Trent a letter outlining the reasons why he should contribute $100 to the community chest, and you may get $10. Have him attend a rally at which he will hear a crippled child and a nurse make their appeals, and he will write the $100 check forthwith. Food and drink are similar auxiliaries. Humor, enthusiasm, energy, courage, and faith are the best of all insubstantial additions to the problem equation.

Solutions to problems in human relations are sometimes brought out of deadlocks by such auxiliary devices as ad hoc committees, acting appointments, and impartial arbitrators.

You are the mayor of a small city. Plans for the building of a new courthouse have been completed. The opposition newspaper charges that the whole project has been handled unwisely. You can ignore the charge. Then many of the readers of the paper will believe the charge. You can write a letter to the paper and deny the charge. But since it is not specific, you have nothing definite to refute. And in a letter to a newspaper you cannot go into all the details. If, however, you appoint a temporary committee to review the handling of the project and report publicly, you will indicate at once your own confidence in the outcome of such a review, and yet you will make no permanent change in the way you carry on the affairs of the city.

Talking over a problem with someone who is not involved in it does not always occur to people who are at loggerheads. Yet the success of nondirective counselors and labor mediators rests to an important degree on the fact that they are neutrals—zero factors—auxiliaries—in the actual problem.

Auxiliaries are devices that aid in the solution of problems though they are not originally part of it. Substitution of one factor for another—women for men workers—is one example of this technique. Adding a new element—keels on boats—is another. Adding a temporary element—a scaffolding during construction or a mediator in a labor dispute—is a third. Imaginative attacks on difficult problems often use auxiliaries whose usefulness in connection with the problem had not previously been noted.

• • •

Find examples of the three types of auxiliaries in your past experience. Which of your examples is the most ingenious? . . . Explore several of your current problems. As you look at each one, reduce to letters the factors that you can manipulate. Now search for X—a wholly new factor that you can add in order to influence the outcome. Review the three kinds of auxiliaries discussed in this chapter. As you do, substitute factors relevant to your problem to stand for X under each kind of auxiliary. Make this an exercise in imagination; try to find substitutes, new elements, and temporary elements that you have not used before. How often do you invent X-factors?

14

Restructuring

❧ *Pull the stocking inside out* ❧

ONE of my mother's favorite reminders when I was a small boy was, "There's more than one way to skin a cat." This bit of folk wisdom would be trotted out when I tried to solve problems such as how to drag on the long stockings kids then wore. Her trick was to turn the stocking inside out, place my foot in the foot of it, and pull the rest on over my foot. It was the reverse of pulling a stocking off. Instead of thrusting the foot down the length of the stocking against resistance that did not have to be met, you simply put your foot where it had to go and easily slipped the stocking over it.

After the battle of Gettysburg Lee's army of 60,000 faced Meade's army of 90,000. According to the book Meade fought by, he could not attack Lee because two men on defense equalled three on offense. He had to have better odds. Abraham Lincoln thought over this stalemate a while. Then he pulled the stocking inside out. "All right," he said in effect to Meade, "so you can't attack. Then you are just as much on the defensive now as Lee is. If the ratio for defense is to 2 to 3, then you need only 40,000 men to defend Washington against Lee's 60,000. That releases 50,000 of your men to harass the enemy elsewhere."

Lincoln and my mother used the same problem-solving technique —they restructured the problem. Changing the structure of a problem is often the technique that succeeds when all else has failed.

102

RESTRUCTURING

The simplest way to restructure a problem is to change your way of looking at it. You do change the problem because the problem exists (for you) only as it seems to you. The only problem you are likely to solve is the one you think you have to solve. Meade thought his problem was offensive. Therefore he was baffled. He could not act. He cried for thousands more of nonexistent Union troops in order to attack. When Lincoln visualized Meade's role at that moment as defensive, he altered the nature of the problem. Then Meade had enough men for that purpose, and 50,000 more to carry out the long-range offensive.

A fisherman and the summer resident of an island off the coast of New England faced the problem of getting the city man, his wife, small child, and baggage aboard the fisherman's boat during a September blow. The boat was two hundred yards offshore, and the gale was blowing onshore at a quartering angle. The fisherman chose to row the wife and child out first and then return for the man and the baggage. By tremendous effort, he reached his boat. After a rest he rowed back to shore in the empty dory. "We'll never make it," he said gloomily. "I just can't make a second trip with you and all them bags."

"I'll tell you what we'll do," said the city man, "I'll row you." He had the flabbergasted fisherman drag the dory a few hundred yards down the shore. Then using the quartering thrust of the waves and the wind to aid him, he guided the dory out to the fisherman's boat, swiftly and without exertion.

To the fisherman the problem was to get from A, the point at which the baggage was piled and the dory was beached, to B, his boat offshore. The city man restructured the problem in this way: The problem is not to get from A to B; it is to get to B. It would be much easier to get to B from C. Therefore I shall move the starting point to C.

According to Chester I. Barnard the only way to break through a

103

complete impasse is to change your purpose. Change of purpose, he says, changes the "environment" of a problem.

Mr. Winter, a Wall Street broker, had trouble with his health, his personal finances, and his business. He dieted, budgeted, and took courses at night. His troubles continued. When he finally faced the question, "What is my purpose in life?", he decided that he disliked Wall Street and wanted to spend his days out of doors. For the past twenty years he has been happy and healthy taking care of gardens in the Catskills. He literally changed the environment of his problem.

A small university faced serious difficulties. The trustees sought the solution in a series of meetings. Boiled down, four possible answers seemed all they had—and none seemed the right answer. They might change the administration. That would not be easy. The president was too old to fire and not old enough to retire. Anyway, the trustees were as responsible for the state of affairs as the president, and it would do little good to fire themselves. They might add some new attraction—a medical school or something like that. But any attraction they could think of would require bales of money. They might raise money. But their efforts in the past had been too feeble for hope there. A miracle might happen. But none had happened, and no portents were in the skies.

The trustees were at the end of their rope. Then they restructured the problem. Instead of asking, "How can we preserve the university?" they asked, "How can we preserve the educational service to youth that was the reason for the university in the first place?" For that problem there did exist a solution. They affiliated with the state university.

Here is an example from American history: After winning independence from Britain in the Revolutionary War, the United States of America became badly disunited and nearly fell apart under the Continental Congress. Problems multiplied, and no one had solutions. The nation had debts but no way to pay them.

Worthless paper money gave us the phrase "not worth a Continental." In Massachusetts Captain Daniel Shay led an armed rebellion. General Washington called a last-ditch meeting at Annapolis, but several of the states were too skeptical or indifferent to send delegates. As the meeting dragged to a close with nothing accomplished, Alexander Hamilton restructured the problem. He took the floor and proposed discarding the old government and building a completely new one out of the same thirteen original states. His words led to the Constitutional Congress of 1787 in Independence Hall and ultimately to the adoption of our present Constitution in 1789.

A common restructuring situation is one in which you cannot meet all conditions of a problem as originally stated. Suppose you are trying to hire a mechanical engineer with experience in the aviation industry. After much screening of candidates, you find that you must choose one of three men. Dennis is a good mechanical engineer with a fair amount of experience in the aviation industry. Chester is a first-rate mechanical engineer with no experience in aviation. Scargo is an industrial engineer with aviation experience. None of these men fits the job specifications perfectly. But those specifications are general and may not be rigid. Perhaps Dennis has excellent sales connections and can be used in ways not contemplated. Perhaps Chester's superior qualities as a mechanical engineer far outweigh his lack of experience in aviation, and vice versa for Scargo.

If you hire one of these men, you have only in a literal sense changed your purpose. You have achieved a satisfactory solution by altering the conditions of the problem in a permissible way. You follow this technique every time you change a deadline—when you decide, for instance, that the annual report you have been writing for several weeks will be just as valuable in the middle of January as on the first and that the extra time will allow you to do a better job without undue pressure.

In another sense restructuring a problem involves manipulating the elements of which it is constructed. Cyrus caused his army to cross the Gyndes River dryshod by cutting a new channel behind the army. My son and I used to play badminton. But we found that beating up a dollar's worth of birds a day made the game too expensive. Then for the feathered birds we substituted golf practice balls made of wool. The game we had then was not badminton, but it was faster, cheaper, and just as much fun. Thomas Stearns, a lawyer, could not keep up with the volume of reading he had to do. He could not reduce the volume, he could not devote more time to reading, and he could not have anyone else read for him. He went to a reading clinic and increased his reading speed.

When the Caxton Corporation was young, it ran into great difficulty in meeting competition. It then manufactured only one product, the Caxton valve. The whole management team tackled the central problem of trimming costs. Still they could not lower their price to the point where they could lure enough buyers away from the leaders in their field. Then the directors shrewdly bought the Peerless Brake plant across the street. Greater facilities and expanded operations resulted in control of costs superior to anything that could be achieved for one product.

In this case the total structure within which the problem (reduction of costs of the Caxton valve) existed was deliberately altered, and the various factors that were part of the original problem were dispersed among those of the new and larger "environment."

You will sometimes find that you can restructure a problem by rearranging the elements in the problem as it is stated. You may literally rearrange the people, objects, words, or symbols, just as you do in jigsaw puzzles. One writer I know types every paragraph of his first draft on a separate sheet of paper. Then he can reorganize his thoughts with a minimum of retyping. In your rearranging of the elements of your problem you may on occasions make your moves at random in search of a clue to a new structure. Or you may follow the logic of a particular system. A tangled length of string can best be unraveled by patiently drawing out the loops, for instance. The mathematician Polya calls this process *decomposing and recombining.* He gives the following as an example:

Problem: Form one word from the anagram DRY OXTAIL IN REAR.

Instead of stabbing away at this problem wildly or spending weeks checking through an unabridged dictionary, Polya arranges an equivalent restatement of the problem:

Form one fifteen-letter word from the following vowels and consonants: AA E II Y O; D L N RRR T X.

According to Polya, people find the answer much more quickly this way. It is "extraordinarily."

Transposition is commonplace in sports. Coaches are always juggling team line-ups. In your daily problems you might get better answers sometimes when you are balked if you study the arrangement of the factors in your problem and then rearrange them as though they were the batting order of a baseball team or counters on a checker board. Suppose you symbolize the factors in one of your problems by *ABCDEF.* This pattern does not work. Therefore you change the order of factors. When you transpose *F* to follow *B,* better results follow.

You probably do not use the rearrangement-of-factors technique as much as you might because the factors do not seem interchangeable or seem so much alike that transposition is pointless.

When we were deciding to buy our house, the principal objection was that it was on the downslope of a hill. The living room on the front of the house, therefore, had no view. The bedroom on the back of the house had a splendid view. It was not at all apparent that these rooms were interchangeable. But once we arrived at the idea that the living room could be used as a bedroom and vice versa, we saw how we could be happy in the house, and we bought it.

Here is how this process of restructuring by decomposing and rearrangement can apply to a business problem:

You are a director of a large industrial training program. Morris and Cassell are not as satisfactory instructors as the other foremen. But they are old hands who know well what they are teaching, and they cannot be replaced. There seems no way in which transposition enters into this problem. But what are the factors? Apart from Morris and Cassell, the factors are the groups of men in training and the processes being taught. Morris and Cassell cannot be switched in any meaningful way. And all the men have to be taught the same processes. What about the men? Following this lead, you test the men and reassign them to Morris and Cassell on the basis of aptitude. Facing groups of evenly distributed skills, Morris and Cassell are much more effective in their instruction.

The factors add up to the same total. They are simply transposed to a different arrangement.

Your solution of any problem in a sense always involves restructuring. It is automatic if not intentional. Every action you take changes the shape of the problem in some manner. Every forward pass thrown in a football game will yield a gain or a loss. Every no-gain is a loss, for the offense has reduced its opportunity to score by one play. How can you use this knowledge? Let's say that you have chosen your course of action. You take your first step. Then you stop. No matter how neatly you have planned all the other steps, you stop. You ask: "What have been the consequences of this step? Has the pattern of the whole problem changed significantly? Does the basic solution still apply? Or should changes be made?"

When you restructure a problem, you change your point of view toward it. You can sometimes change your point of view by trying to see your problem as the other fellow sees it. You can ask other people to tell you how they see it. You can change your physical point of view—get out of your office and walk around the shop, leave Rochester and take a boat down the St. Lawrence. You can change your psychological point of view. By putting your problem aside until you are rested, unhurried, and cheerful, you may get a fresh grip on it, ask new questions about it, take a livelier interest in it. It is then a new problem.

Restructuring is a basic technique of problem solving. (1) Change of point of view, (2) permissible change of objective, or (3) rearrangement of the elements of a problem provide alternatives not apparent in the original statement.

• • •

Take a problem that you have worked on for some time and that has you stumped. See if you can restructure it. First, walk around it and have another look at it from all sides as though you have never seen it before. Study your written statement of the problem. Imagine that you are another person involved in the problem. Rewrite the statement, using different key terms wherever possible. Now go over your statements with an attentive listener. Explain to him the possible differences that changes in the statement may introduce. (By now you may well have discovered one of the two most common roadblocks—a false assumption or an overlooked alternative.) . . .

Reexamine your objective. Is there any way in which it may with propriety be altered? Can you accomplish part of the problem now and be sure to accomplish the rest later—or be permitted to try to do so? . . . If the objective cannot be altered, can you change any of the elements in the problem? Can you make any substitutions?

Rearrange the order of your elements, perhaps their sequence in time. What effect might that have? . . . If you have not found an answer yet, decide how far you can go without committing yourself to a complete course of action. Then proceed, stopping after each move to analyze the changes you are bringing about. . . . Notice that restructuring applies to your problem, not to your efforts to solve the problem. If you are unable to restructure your problem, then you will have to go on exploring further means of solving it as it stands. But the most difficult problems are more likely to yield to restructuring than to any other technique of attack.

Part III

SCIENTIFIC APPROACH

IN THIS third section you shift gears. Up to this point you have been considering various aspects of problem solving of a fairly informal sort. Now you are to consider more formal aspects essential to any organized approach you might call scientific. In your everyday affairs, apart from the actual processes of science, these methods are not difficult to apply. Your efforts to solve your problems are always based on *Hypotheses* of some sort, of which you may or may not be aware. Your efforts will frequently take the form of an *Experiment*, guided by a hypothesis and more or less rigorously controlled. And whether your problem is a simple one or an intricate one, whether you are trying to diagnose your problem or attack it by means of the techniques discussed earlier, you rely every inch of the way on your ability to reason. Now it is time for you to review the simplest elements of *Logic*. Because they are special logical processes much used in problem solving, you will get acquainted with *Analogy* and *Cause and Effect*. Once more, you will see that you cannot expect yourself to memorize these matters and apply them consciously to every problem you meet. But you can expect to deepen your understanding of these formal methods to the point where you recognize when you are using them and then know how to use them correctly.

15

Hypothesis

~ *"What use is a baby?"* ~

ABOUT four centuries before Christ, Hippocrates—author of the Hippocratic oath that doctors to this day swear before they are allowed to practice—expressed his belief that illness was not the work of demons but of natural causes. He gave to the world one of the great hypotheses that have emancipated human beings. Over a thousand years passed before much evidential data supported his hypothesis, and still research goes on tirelessly to isolate the causes of some of our grimmest destroyers. But so long ago Hippocrates released Western civilization from the savage's belief in the alliance of evil spirits and disease. And he put medical science on the self-reliant path of observation and experiment to discover the solutions of its problems.

When William Harvey in 1651 wrote, "Almost all animals, even those which bring forth their young alive, and man himself, are produced from eggs," his statement was in the words of the *Encyclopaedia Britannica* "a prevision of genius." Not until 1827 did Von Baer discover the mammalian ovum and prove Harvey's hypothesis correct. But it is a landmark in medical history.

When Albert Einstein wrote $E = Mc^2$, he gave man's thinking about the structure of the universe he inhabits a revolutionary shift. Spelled out, Einstein's formula means that energy equals mass times

113

THE ART OF PROBLEM SOLVING

the square of the speed of light in centimeters per second. This hypothesis is revolutionary because energy and mass were previously considered qualitatively different and not equatable. Now scientists— and all the young people in schools and colleges—are able to conceive of the dizzy notion that a brick and the energy that propels it through the air are merely variations of one another. And thinking in terms of such extraordinary newness has projected us into the atomic age.

A hypothesis is an informed guess. When Heinrich Schliemann advanced the hypothesis in 1870 that the site of an actual Troy, the city sung by Homer, was Hissarlik in Asia Minor, he was guessing. But Schliemann, though a businessman, had a scholar's knowledge of Homer, and he had studied the Homeric sites at first hand. His guess was an informed one. Excavations confirmed his hypothesis and led to some of the most exciting archaeological discoveries of all time.

A hypothesis is a guess that has some reasonable chance of being right. Lost in a wood, a child will wander blindly, circuitously. A woodsman will use what information he has to figure out the most promising direction in which to walk and the means for continuing in that direction. Or he will figure that his chances for rescue are best if he stays exactly where he is.

A hypothesis is a general assumption that has yet to be proved. It differs from simple assumptions in often being a plan of attack on a problem. Or it seeks to explain why something is the way it is or why under certain conditions it will be some other way. Multitudes of hypotheses are proved false and discarded. Many others, like those of Hippocrates and Harvey, remain unproved one way or the other for long periods. Others, like the axioms on which geometry rests, are assumed to be true. "Self-evident truths" such as the one that parallel lines never meet or that they meet at infinity are not really subject to proof. We go on using them daily just the same with practical results.

HYPOTHESIS

When your hypothesis proves true enough times to convince you that it may be true all the time or with enough frequency to be useful, you indicate your increased certainty by calling it a theory. If it proves true invariably, you have discovered a law.

When you are riding along in your car, you are really being supported and propelled by hundreds of what were once far-fetched hypotheses that finally achieved enough reliability for you to ride on them. You would not dream of calling blood plasma anything but practical. Every hour throughout the world blood transfusions save lives. Yet this boon to mankind had to take form first as a hypothesis. In the course of studying the chemistry of the blood in the laboratories for pure research at the Harvard Medical School a scientist had to say, "It would be highly beneficial if blood could be stored as plasma." So the "mining" of blood began.

The trouble with theorists is not that they make theories, but that some of them make bad theories. Their theories will not work because the authors lack first-hand experience or specialized training or basic intelligence. Yet if your idea of being practical is to throttle your own efforts to speculate freely and imaginatively with hypothetical solutions to problems or if you rebuff the efforts of your associates to do so, you are not likely to solve many important problems.

Speculation is therefore as much a part of problem solving as accumulation and observation of facts. The new instrument the microscope enabled Robert Hooke, the seventeenth-century physicist, to be one of the first men to observe the cellular structure of living organisms. But he did not know what he saw, for the hypothesis of cells did not occur to him or to anybody else until nearly a century later.

Erich Fromm says that creative thinking starts with a "rational vision" and that the analysis of this hypothesis and the gathering of data to support it may lead to a more adequate hypothesis and eventually perhaps to a wide-ranging theory. Conant makes distinctions between a limited working hypothesis helpful in solving an immediate problem; a broad speculative hypothesis like that of Hippocrates', from which more highly organized hypotheses can be evolved; and a working hypothesis on a grand scale—a "conceptual scheme," from which deductions capable of experimental tests can be made. The atomic theory advanced by John Dalton in 1808 is an example of a conceptual scheme.

You will not find it necessary to worry much about the kinds of hypotheses and theories you can use in your problem solving. You will use all kinds at one time or another. The limited working hypothesis—a plan of attack—is the one you will formulate most often. For instance, if you are an insurance company representative assigned to locate a missing beneficiary, you would probably start your search at the last known places of residence and employment.

The worth of a hypothesis is tested by its inclusiveness. The fewer words you use to gather in the ideas you are considering, the better. The educated man's search for ever-wider bases for his decisions leads him back to inclusive hypotheses, even in the solution of simple problems.

Suppose that you are overweight. You consult doctors. You struggle with diets. You keep track of calories. You make resolutions. You break them. You worry. Food and your weight obsess you. How can a look at your hypothesis help you? First, you know you must have one. You cannot make an effort to solve any problem without a plan—a hypothesis—of some sort. In this case perhaps your hypothesis is too limited. Perhaps you are guided only by a belief that you would be more comfortable and better looking if you could reduce. This attack on the problem is grounded in vanity. Now you look around for a hypothesis of wider scope. You see that your being overweight jeopardizes your health, and you see that you are therefore putting your family's welfare in jeopardy. You now construct a much more inclusive hypothesis: My devotion to my family requires me to stick to the diet my doctor prescribes.

116

When a problem is not working out satisfactorily, you may well ask yourself: "What hypothesis underlies my plan of attack? Does it make my approach understandable and justifiable? Can I find a broader concept to guide me? Can I find one that embraces all others and is linked with a fundamental philosophy?" In many situations your decisions will be good or mediocre solely on the basis of your ability to select from competing hypotheses the one with the greatest scope.

Yet you make a constructive attack on a problem when you advance a reasonable hypothesis, even though it may prove wrong. Toward the end of the eighteenth-century Allessandro Volta of Padua set out to prove by experiment that Luigi Galvani's hypothesis of animal magnetism was sound. He ended by inventing the electric battery. And during the third quarter of the nineteenth-century the French scientist Louis Pasteur and a German chemist named Liebig had a prolonged controversy on the nature of fermentation. Neither was right. Further research has led to an understanding of the catalytic action of enzymes, about which neither Pasteur nor Liebig was informed. But their hypotheses formulated the problem so that later scientists could advance to the correct solution.

How do you go about finding a hypothesis? One basis for setting up a hypothesis on which you can proceed with your efforts to solve a problem is analogy with similar problems. Another is observation. Informed guesses often follow perception of (1) a pattern or system in whatever is being studied, or (2) a deviation from a known pattern.

The study of the history of language was an unscientific affair up until 1822. By then Rasmus Rask and Jacob Grimm observed in their study of many ancient and modern languages a regularity in the changes during the centuries. They saw, for instance, that the Latin p and t as in *pater* regularly became f and th as in the English *father*. The hypothesis that started with these observations of regularity in pattern became Grimm's Law, which has been enormously helpful in making philology a science.

Observation of deviations from a pattern—from the expected way things go—can also lead to a useful hypothesis. For instance, to carry on the previous illustration, Karl Verner observed many exceptions to Grimm's Law until he finally was able to perceive a regular stress shift and so unite these exceptions in a pattern. His hypothesis is now Verner's Law to linguists.

You will find some of your most brilliant solutions come from hypotheses based on the connection of the remote with the immediate—on the application of a general idea to a particular problem when no obvious connection exists.

In 1928 a young scholar named Garland sought the advice of Professor Ashley H. Thorndike about the desirability of putting aside his doctoral research in order to undertake a remunerative editorial assignment in a publishing venture. Thorndike was a distinguished literary scholar, not an economist. He gazed out of his office window a while, then said: "Well, Garland, you had better stick to your research. One of these days we might have another panic. If we do, speculative publishing will stop right away." The next year came the crash of 1929. The publisher closed up shop among the first. Ashley Thorndike had been able to sense in the events of the booming twenties a general theoretical danger and to apply that hypothesis to the solution of a personal problem.

The solution of many of your problems must follow a multiple-hypotheses approach. You cannot afford to be satisfied with only one hypothesis on which to base your efforts. You list all the relevant possibilities and then eliminate them one by one. When one hypothesis seems promising, you still ask, "Will another hypothesis apply equally well?"

The classic example of the multiple-hypotheses approach is the murder mystery. Did Mrs. Derringer murder her elderly husband, Caleb Derringer, because of another love? Did the ne'er-do-well

Philip Derringer do the deed before his father could change his will and disinherit him? Or could it have been Caleb Derringer's schizophrenic half-sister, Birdy Manton? What about the secretive Dunraven, Derringer's butler-secretary, who had the power of attorney? And the mysterious woman with the French accent who visited him the night of the murder? By testing each hypothesis in turn the Scotland Yard inspector proves who did murder the unfortunate Caleb Derringer.

To use a hypothesis effectively in the solution of a problem, you must first be clear what it is. Every course of action rests on some sort of hypothesis, as I have said. For instance, behind all the specific proposals of an architect in planning a schoolhouse lies the modern theory of functionalism—that he must use his knowledge of design, engineering, and materials to create a more efficient and pleasant environment for children and teachers. Thus, when you examine your own or somebody else's proposed solution, you ask, "Why are we doing this?"—in other words, "What hypothesis underlies the suggested action?" You might say your hypotheses make your strategy.

Next you must test your hypothesis without prejudice. Your attitude must be one of suspended judgment. The testing of a large percentage of your ideas must be by discussion. Time, expense, and the consequences of the action often make a practical test of a hypothesis before a final decision not feasible. Your routine procedure then takes the form of accepting hypothetically one theory after another while you explore its implications for possible solutions. You say in effect: "We see where Dick's idea would lead us. It sounds pretty expensive, but let's not make up our minds about it until we have a look at Frank's and Paul's."

Because it is not always easy to visualize the potential value in speculative ideas, it is desirable to have a person who has faith in a hypothesis present it. Once you find a hypothesis that seems workable, try to knock it down with the same dispassionate energy that you explored it for its positive contributions to the solution of your

119

problem. What would happen if this occurred? Does it take care of that eventuality? How would it affect this operation? You borrow a bit of the glory of the scientific spirit every time you examine your ideas in this objective way.

Of course, if the hypothesis is one that you can put to an actual test without too much expense or without unfortunate consequence if it fails, then testing is your best procedure. Often, however, there can be no protected test for your hypothesis. Unless it works, something unpleasant happens. Giving it a stiff analytical going over before you put it into practice is your best insurance.

The practical importance of a usable new hypothesis can hardly be overestimated. Collection of more and more facts, the passion for research and statistical data, cannot take the place of a simple idea that directs action in new and more productive channels of problem solving. An enlightened guess may save years of wrong-directioned activity. The value of secret data about a country for which spies risk their lives is trivial compared with a sound hypothesis that political pressures will force the leaders to behave in a certain way.

Solving problems when hard beset, said Justice Benjamin Cordozo, is accomplished by the "flash of a luminous hypothesis," followed by the "successive stages of preparation, incubation, and illumination." Hypotheses are your eyes as you try to approach problems in a scientific manner. Through them you look into the disorder that is a problem and see the possibilities of order. To the practical man who scoffs at theories you can quote Disraeli's definition of a practical man— one who can be counted on to perpetuate the mistakes of his ancestors. Or you can say to him what Ben Franklin said to the man in Paris who asked, "What use is a balloon?" "What use is a baby?" retorted Ben.

•   •   •

Review your thinking about a few of your past problems. What hypotheses did you consider for each? Which did you act on? How sound were your educated guesses? Have you accepted any of them as general theories or laws to be applied to other problems? . . . Now study a difficult problem that you are working on at present. Isolate the main hypothesis on which you are proceeding or planning to proceed. You can reduce it to a short statement like, "If I expand my business, I'll make more money than I am making now." Now you have only two questions to answer: (1) Is this hypothesis really sound? (2) Can you think of a more fruitful one—especially a more inclusive one—that will indicate a different course of action? For instance, the second question might lead to this substitute for the sample hypothesis: "If I expand my business, I will not have time to live sensibly." . . . Select a problem situation—a situation where something is wrong but you have no specific problem isolated. See how many hypotheses you can advance to explain this situation. Let yourself go and remember that you are trying to find new ways of looking at a set of facts—you are not at the moment concerned about making your theories work.

16

Experiment

He got dead pigeons

THE unicorn, a legendary beast with one horn, was highly prized in the fifteenth and sixteenth centuries. Queen Elizabeth's Horn of Windsor was valued at one-half million dollars. Not only its rarity but also its marvelous prophylactic power made the horn of this fabulous animal precious: it could render poison harmless and cure many diseases. Then the court physician of Catherine de' Medici decided to see for himself. He fed pigeons arsenic and powdered "unicorn" horn—and got dead pigeons. Then investigation of the source of the supply of the merchants of Copenhagen revealed that the horn was only the tusk of the narwhal.

The management of the Chandler Hotel had debated a good deal about keeping the coffee shop open after 8:00 P.M. and had collected several batches of statistics and opinions—all of which indicated not enough potential customers at that time to make the venture profitable. The manager of the Chandler decided to end the debate by opening the shop on a trial basis. The move was a success. What was not evident—and could not be proved or disproved in advance—was that in that section of the city at night there were many people who wished the type of restaurant service offered by a good hotel coffee shop. The experimental opening of the shop brought them together and threw out the statistics and guessing.

122

EXPERIMENT

"Let's try it and see what will happen" solves many a problem. It is one of the main streets of the scientific approach.

All experience is experimental. The truths of science and old wives' tales are equally subject to revision by day-to-day testing. The boy tinkering with a Model T in a woodshed is as richly endowed with the experimental attitude as the Ph.D. occupant of a cubicle in a research center. The business woman of forty who decides to spend her vacation hosteling through Europe on a bicycle instead of hotel-ing in the Catskills, the fifth-grade teacher who takes her children to visit a house while it is being built, the housewife who wants to find out what would happen if she added chives to the mayonnaise, the store executive who puts Miss Dobbs in charge of home furnishings in order to give her a chance to show what she can do—these are all experimentalists.

Trial and error is the simplest form of experimentation. It is also the most usual of human and animal problem-solving techniques.

The fastest and best method of finding the answer to a simple problem is often through trial and error. This axiom is disputed by many women, who think talking about it is more interesting, and by many men, who think they should refer it to a committee. How to get the most books of unassorted sizes into a carton can best be determined by picking them up and fitting them in. Only timing various ways will tell you which is the fastest way to fold 1000 sheets of paper down the middle by hand. The way to find out how the furniture in your living room looks best to you is to move it about and observe the effects. In a machine shop rejection of parts that do not fit during assembly is often quicker and less expensive than inspecting each part as it is made.

Trial and error is a respectable part of our knowledge in many fields. Cooking, farming, weather predicting, and building today depend on the records of the trials, errors, and successes of distant yesterdays. The alchemists of the dark ages who attempted to change base metals into gold by mixing fantastic messes of liquids and solids and gases led the way to the ultimate discovery of standard chemical combinations. The maps and charts that record advances in geographical knowledge are based on countless explorations and reports from the earliest timid voyagers to Admiral Byrd. The recorders worked in the dark or were badly misled by current theories, but the information they garnered led to clearer hypotheses and more systematic investigations. The laws of nations and the customs and policies of organized groups of all kinds have a high practicability content—they exist because they have been tried and found to work.

Nevertheless, the staggering quantity of unsolved problems and of problems that went unsolved for long periods while trial and error failed to produce the right answers suggests that trial and error as a system has some flaw. The trouble with it is that it is generally practiced with the eyes shut. Random trial-and-error efforts often are no more productive than those of a bumble bee to get through a screen door. They represent the same low-level automatic response and satisfy the same desire to be doing something that doubtless stirs the bee. In human society a good deal of such effort is designed to forestall criticism by superiors, fellow workers, and conscience and to be a substitute for the burdensome effort of reasoning.

Here is an illustration of the futility of random experiment, supplied by Professor Victor Goedicke: "Every puzzle enthusiast has probably tried to solve the popular 'burr' puzzle, consisting of six notched blocks of wood which must be fitted together to form a three-dimensional cross. The puzzle is popular because people believe that, since there are only six pieces, it should be easy to solve simply by trying all of the possible arrangements until the right one is found. A little elementary permutation theory will show how misguided this effort is: Relative to any given starting block, the second block can have any of five possible positions, and corresponding to each of these, the third block can have any of four positions, and so forth. But any block can be inserted into its position in any of eight ways—it can be laid on any of its four sides or turned end for end and again laid on any of its four sides. The total number of arrangements which it would be necessary to try is therefore 5 x 4 x 3 x 2 x 8 to the sixth power, or 1,351,680. If a trial-and-error solver could perform one trial per minute and worked an eight-hour day, he could try all of the possibilities in something over seven years—assuming that he had the good luck not to repeat experiments he had already tried. I have never seen anyone solve this puzzle by trial and error."

Trial and error need not be random. An element of selectivity or a pattern may be introduced. Mrs. Peters discovered when she reached her car that she had lost her car keys in the sand by the ocean. She returned to the spot where she had been sitting. Hours of random combing the deep sand might have been in vain, but a systematic crisscross search dug the keys out in ten minutes. This grid system is the one used by our planes on searches for submarines and on similar patrols. It is still a trial-and-error affair, but it is made more efficient by a formula. Of course, efforts may be highly organized and still be senseless trial and error—the so-called systems followed by gamblers, for instance.

To use trial and error productively as a problem-solving technique, therefore, you should have hypotheses and records to guide you. Otherwise, you will not be able to check your successes and failures and may hit on the right answer without knowing what method you used. It is not easy to hit accidentally on the right way to park a car between two other cars. And having finally succeeded by turning the wheel this way and that, you are not any wiser the next time. As in the solution of puzzles, you can do much better by trying out one tentative solution at a time and noting exactly which method works.

Experimentation by testing samples is more truly scientific.

To find out whether or not the colors in a certain kind of cloth are waterproof, you would put a piece of it in a bowl of water. If the colors of the sample do not run, the colors in that make of cloth are fast. If the colors in the sample do run, the colors in that make of cloth are not fast. This simple example represents much of the vast activity of solving problems experimentally. It also represents the two points you have to check with care.

1. Is the sample truly representative? By error or fraud, the piece of cloth tested might not come from the cloth under consideration. Or the larger piece from which it is taken may not be representative of the regular product. So it is in problems of human relations. Business leaders sometimes get erroneous ideas about their problems because they talk to atypical employees or customers.

2. Is the test what it purports to be? Through accident, carelessness, or deceit, the liquid in the bowl might not be pure water. In order to guard against these two sources of trouble, you have to set up controls over your experiments. The assignment of identical hands to different players in duplicate bridge is a controlled situation. This device rules out the chance factor in the original deal and makes possible fairer comparison of the skill of the players.

A classic example of a controlled experiment is Reed's on yellow fever. In 1900 Cuba was full of yellow fever. Many of our soldiers had died from it during the Spanish-American War, and others had brought it to the United States. The generally accepted theory was that yellow fever was contracted from "fomites"—the soiled and bloody bedding and clothing of fever victims. Dr. Carlos Finlay of Havana had another hypothesis. He thought that mosquitoes were the agents for spreading the disease.

Then Dr. Walter Reed and his heroic volunteers carried out their historic experiment at Quemados. In one building three volunteers, protected from mosquitoes, slept for three weeks in the bedclothing of victims who had died of yellow fever. They did not contract the disease. In another building volunteers who slept in clean beds but were exposed to the bites of infected mosquitoes did contract yellow fever. The experiment was conclusive.

To control an experiment in a laboratory, you often carry out tests with two or more groups. The units of the first group—mice, pieces of steel, or what not—would all be alike. The units of the second group would all be similar to those in the first group except in one respect. And so on. If every piece of steel in group A breaks under certain pressure and all of the pieces in group B, the same as group A except for the addition of alloy Z, withstand much greater pressure, you have sufficient evidence of the effect of alloy Z. The value of conducting your experiment with a large number of identical units is that you further exclude the accidental. If you have only one or two pieces of steel in each group, for instance, you would have no safeguard against the misleading results that would follow a mistake in the reading of the pressure gauge.

The isolation of one or more factors that are dependably present—common denominators or constants—is a prime aim of much experiment. In his definitive treatise on the headache Dr. Harold G. Wolff reports on the records of thousands of cases. Among these thousands are many who share several symptoms. This collection of constants or common denominators—technically called a syndrome—marks the migraine type. Not every member of the migraine type has all of the same symptoms as all other members. But each member shares enough of the symptoms shown by the other members to be classified within the type.

You will use known factors as constants in another standard way in your experiments. For example, at Purdue University the agriculture department is searching for new sources of food for hogs. With each new substance, not known to have food value (though as a reasonable hypothesis it may have), the hogs are fed a food known to be beneficial. This is the constant. The basic experimental formula, therefore, can be written A (the known constant) plus X, Y, or Z (the unknowns). The constant A keeps the hogs in good health. If at any time the hogs gain weight, the variable (X, Y, or Z) must be the cause.

The experimental attitude is first of all one of generous open-mindedness to new ideas and hard-headed insistence on putting them to proof by test. If you are imbued with the experimental attitude, you have an underlying faith that there is always a better way of doing things. You reject the tacit assumption of the slothful, the dull in spirit, and the reactionary and assume that your problems and the problems of society are never completely solved, are always capable of improvement. This is the philosophy underlying American progress. It is the unit that makes what we call free enterprise dynamic.

When George Tinnerman invented an ingenious self-locking nut-and-screw combination, he immediately made his patent available to his competitors. He explained this action to his startled associates in this way: "If we protect ourselves with this patent, we will sit tight and not do a thing to improve it. Then our competitors will be forced to come up with something better, and we will be left behind. But if we make this patent available to them, then we know that we have to keep making it better to stay ahead, and we will."

The experimental attitude involves not merely optimism but fearlessness—the courage to face the consequences of experimental activities. In a world mad about security it is perhaps quixotic to champion an attitude that seems deliberately to cultivate insecurity. And while improvements come about through experiment, the tentativeness about the experimental attitude and the willingness not to rest but to push on to new solutions are not conducive to ease or tranquillity.

When you use the experimental approach to your problem solving, you commit yourself to a formula something like this: You start with a hypothesis that you tentatively assume to be true. Then you ruthlessly try through your experiment to secure enough converging evidence to prove that it is true or that it is not. If it is unsatisfactory, you remodel it or discard it and construct a new concept and carry out another experiment. When your conclusion is "true," you accept it as also tentative and subject to further verification or overthrow.

In everyday affairs your experiments are not all conducted under strictly controlled conditions. They do not need to be. Experiments in human relations rarely permit controlled situations. Neither people nor conditions can be exactly duplicated, though close duplications can be managed and trusted within narrow ranges. But a good problem solver values an experiment that does not work. He counts the proof of negative results a positive gain—something to guide him and keep him from error in the future. Whether you conduct a controlled laboratory type of experiment or put your ideas to the touchstone of actual trial without the paraphernalia of controlled conditions and precise records, you will be attacking your problems in a scientific spirit when you say, "Let's try it and see what happens."

• • •

Select a problem in which you are using an experimental approach. Are you proceeding by trial and error? If so, is it random? If not, what hypothesis is guiding you? What records of methods used and of success and failure are you keeping? Is any pattern emerging from your efforts? . . . If you are running controlled experiments, then are your samples representative? Are the conditions of your tests what they are supposed to be? Answering these questions requires first-hand checking. . . . How about your own attitude toward your problem? Are you suspending judgment while you observe closely the results of your various tests? Or are you so sure that you know the right answer that you are not following the evidence with an open mind? Are you alert to accept the results of your tests if they run counter to your assumptions? . . . If you are not at present trying to solve a problem by experimental means, perhaps you can give yourself experience in the use of the method by comparing the results of the method you now use to handle a recurrent problem with those of another method that may be better. In other words run a controlled experiment on one of your problem-solving methods.

129

17

Logic

You probably have heard the argument for the health fad of drinking milk in the form of yogurt: The Bulgarians are famous for good health and longevity. They drink yogurt. If you drink yogurt, you will also be healthy and live long. Faddists invariably defend their notions by a show of logic. You must have doubts that the health and longevity of the Bulgarians can be caused by one item in their diet—especially when American scientists report that yogurt is not any healthier than ordinary milk, which is cheaper.

For your problem diagnosis or attack to be scientific, your constant duty is to determine (1) whether or not statements are true and (2) what inferences may properly be drawn from them. The scientific approach to problem solving is always by way of the path of logic.

Enders may in truth be a fine speaker, a member of many organizations working for the public good, and a devoted husband and father. The inference that he is therefore qualified to be mayor of the city does not follow. McGlug may have a criminal record extending back to the robbery of another child's piggy bank at the age of four. That he is in truth the kind of man who robs banks does not make it true that he robbed the Natchez Bank and Trust Company on May 13. That it has rained during the past thirteen days of July in Florida is true. It does not follow that it rains nearly fifty per cent of the time in Florida. That political corruption is common in some Latin American countries is true. It does not follow that the best way to do business in São Paolo is to try bribing the mayor.

Logic enjoys a reputation for problem solving that stretches all the way back to Aristotle. Yet in spite of its great prestige, few people seem able to reason logically, and fewer yet seem disposed to accept conclusions arrived at logically unless they coincide with conclusions previously reached emotionally. As part of your experience in problem solving, you will have to take for granted that human beings are not logical. They cannot be counted on to behave in a certain way because you are able to demonstrate that it is the reasonable way. You will instead have to count on the nonrational behavior of people and the great importance of the emotional element in their reactions as part of the equation in solving most problems.

Nevertheless, logic gives you mighty leverage on problems. Without it you are as helpless as Samson shorn of his hair, and like Samson you are liable to solve your problems by bringing the roof down on your own head. Decision making deals with probabilities. Whether or not you put your faith in one probability or another depends on your ability to reason about the supporting evidence. The evidence may be sound, but you may add it up wrong. Other people may add up the evidence right or wrong, and you may make a poor estimate of the degree of credibility of their conclusions. Mastery of logic enables you to get a hold on a difficult problem much as a skilled wrestler puts an armlock or a half nelson on an opponent. But you need not be a master of the technicalities to understand some of the major operations of logic in the solution of problems. You do not have to be a logician to be logical. But sound logic means sound decisions.

Let us therefore take a look at some of the logical processes that will be most useful to you. If the going gets rough, hang on. The main ideas are simple enough. You use them every day.

The major forms of reasoning are *deductive* and *inductive*. Some authorities add *inductive-deductive* as a separate form.

131

THE ART OF PROBLEM SOLVING

In *deduction* you reason that whatever is true of all instances or members of a class must be true of one instance or member. In *induction* you reason that what is true of a sufficient number of instances or members of a class must be true of all. You will use a *combination of the two* forms in solving most of your problems.

The simple use of pure *deduction* in the solution of a problem is easy. All telephone calls for Mr. Fotherington must be referred to Miss Stanhope. That is an order issued to the switchboard operators. Whenever a call for Mr. Fotherington comes through, each operator unconsciously goes through the following steps: (1) All telephone calls for Mr. Fotherington must be referred to Miss Stanhope. (2) This is a telephone call for Mr. Fotherington. (3) This telephone call must be referred to Miss Stanhope. These are the classic steps of deductive reasoning. They make up what is called a syllogism.

You can see the beautiful inevitability of deduction. Once you can make that first statement—the major premise—with assurance, you have the answer for any single instance that comes within its limits. Whatever is true of *all* telephone calls to Mr. Fotherington *must* be true of this telephone call to him. The geometry of Euclid (c. 300 B.C.) is the highest triumph of deductive reasoning. For instance, Euclid established that the square of the hypotenuse of a right-angled triangle is equal to the sum of the squares of the other two sides. Surveyors to this day are able confidently to map out Farmer Nickerson's back pasture for building lots because the triangles there are subject to the same laws as all other triangles.

You might say that we try to arrange our problems so that as many of them as possible can be solved deductively. All westbound passenger trains leaving Norwalk stop at New York. Having accepted the truth of this premise, the Norwalk commuter stands on the westbound platform reading his paper and steps on the first passenger train that comes in without asking the conductor what its destination is. Lawyer Cameron has driven from his home in Centerville to the county seat at Zenith for years. He always makes the best time by following Route 6, he says.

Now you begin to see the limits of deduction. To be the sure-fire problem solver it seems at first, it must have a major premise that is *without exception* true. At some time or other Route 6 will be under repair or otherwise impassable. Then Lawyer Cameron will have to make an exception to his "always." A special chartered train might not stop at New York. And if Mrs. Fotherington called up, perhaps Mr. Fotherington would expect the telephone operator to connect her directly with him—or perhaps he would the next time.

As soon as your major premise loses its absolutely-so truth and takes on an almost-always-true quality, when like the Captain in Gilbert and Sullivan's *Pinafore* you switch from "never" to "hardly ever," then the cutting edge of your logic is dulled. If you cannot say absolutely that every snake in Morgan County is nonpoisonous, then this snake may be poisonous. If you cannot say that all errors in the manufacture of a certain drug by your pharmaceutical supply firm will be caught before the distribution of the pills, you may endanger the lives of many thousands of people, since pills may be produced in runs of a million.

But, you say, in life we have to take many roads that we have excellent reason to believe the best—we have to act on many premises that we cannot guarantee to be without exception. We act on the reasonable assumption that something or other is always true. Yes, we do. But then we are no longer using deductive logic with ironbound inevitability.

Here, in fact, is exactly where many people work their way into problems and fail to work themselves out again. They make two simple logical mistakes and fall into two traps.

The fellow who takes somebody's remark that there are no poisonous snakes in Morgan County in a literal sense and then is bitten by one of the few copperheads still about has made the mistake of taking a statement of what is generally true to have an absolute meaning. This is trap one—to accept a generalization as always true, when it is only almost always true or always true as far as known, and then to apply it to a specific case. That Route 6 has been clear every time Lawyer Cameron has ridden on it during the past twenty years does not prove that it will be clear today when you ride on it.

The person who is told that all common field mushrooms, the *Agaricus campestris*, are edible and then eats a similar looking *Amanita verna*, the "destroying angel," has made a logical (and fatal) error in classification. All common field mushrooms are edible, but the *Amanita verna*, which often grows in fields, is not a common field mushroom. It is not correctly included in the major premise. This is trap two.

Let's go over these two errors again.

1. Men are making fortunes investing in oil companies. If I invest in oil companies, I will make a fortune. The first error is in accepting a generalization as though it were always true when it is not. *All* men who invest in oil companies do not make fortunes.

2. All members of the investment firm of Trowbridge and Adams can be trusted, and therefore Mr. Benjamin can be trusted. Mr. Benjamin, it turns out, is not a member of Trowbridge and Adams: he pretends he is. The second error lies in trying to apply the truth about the general class to an instance that does not belong in that class.

You will find that the inevitability that makes deductive reasoning so irresistible when it is properly applied rarely exists in everyday problems. You can count on the square of the hypotenuse of a right-angled triangle always to be equal to the sum of the squares of the other two sides. But you obviously cannot say with the same absoluteness that all members of a firm can be trusted. Yet to be aware that a general premise is not always true is only part of the game. To decide in a given situation to count on it as true or not true, to act on your judgment, and to have the outcome prove your reasoning sound—that is the quintessence of logic in action.

134

Now let us turn to *induction*. It is the logic underlying all efforts to solve problems by experience and by experiment. By inductive reasoning you reach a general conclusion from a number of instances. How many instances you have to observe before you may safely draw your conclusion depends on your problem. If it is to prove whether or not you can swim the English Channel, one successful attempt is sufficient to establish the general truth that you do have the ability. Neither one nor a hundred successful attempts would prove that you could always swim the English Channel.

If, however, your problem is to determine whether or not drug Zed is beneficial in the treatment of rheumatic fever, one successful treatment would be meaningless. Seven successes might give you grounds to be hopeful. Seventy-two successes might bring you close to certainty—that is, it might if your scorecard read 72—0 and not 72—7 or even 72—1. One failure ruins the *always* you are trying to establish.

You can see immediately that the number of instances necessary to constitute formal proof of a general statement must run from one to millions. Once Magellan sailed around the earth, no other journey was necessary to prove that it could be done. The first pilot who flew a plane faster than the speed of sound proved for all time the theory that it is possible. On the other hand, in establishing theories of heredity, T. H. Morgan and his students have had to carry out experiments involving millions of fruit flies.

The aim of scientific induction is to arrive at general conclusions so invariably true that they may act as major premises for deductive inferences from there on. Scientific experiments are part of an inductive operation aimed at establishing some regularity of behavior that can be called a law.

But you can also see that in the course of solving the ordinary problems of daily existence—not to mention the most difficult ones of relations between human beings—you are going to have to act on the basis of general ideas that do not have and can never have the sort of certainty demanded by science. If Lawyer Cameron has driven the three routes between Centerville and Zenith a dozen times, do you not agree that he has sufficient grounds for acting regularly on the belief that Route 6 is the best? If over a period of two years Mrs. Stiles finds the prices in the Bumble Bee market lower than at the Brown and White and the Ambassador, do you not agree that she has sufficient grounds for trading regularly at the Bumble Bee?

You can see that in both scientific induction and the everyday variety you are concerned with probability. As a scientist you might have to study thousands of instances of a certain grain blight before you could prove that one parasite was the cause of that blight. But you would not need anything like the same number of instances to arrive at a shrewd guess—a hypothesis—that one parasite was probably the cause and go ahead with action to defeat it. Do you see this important distinction? You would try to cure the blight by killing the parasite long before you had certain proof that the parasite was the cause. Once you reach the conviction that a solution is worth trying, you try it. If killing the parasite cures the blight, you have saved valuable time by acting on your hypothesis. Even if you prove your hypothesis wrong, you have still saved time.

Different conditions will demand different *degrees* of probability. If you are buying cord for clotheslines, you might think ten satisfactory samples sufficient to justify a conclusion about the uniformity of its strength. If you are buying the same cord for parachutes, you might wish to test hundreds of pieces. The uniformity of strength required for parachute cords demands a high mathematical expectation that your inference from the instances examined is reliable. The probability that you are right has not the same critical importance for clotheslines.

Just as with deduction, there are two traps for the unwary in the use of the inductive process in solving problems.

1. Have you enough instances to establish the degree of prob-

ability that the circumstances require? Of course, hidden behind that question is the more crucial one: How many do the circumstances require? We have discussed that question at length because of its importance. It puts your judgment to the test every day.

Hasty generalization—coming to a conclusion without sufficient examples—remains one of the commonest sources for the errors that cause problems. Just listen, and all day long you will hear people cite one or two instances and then jump to a whopping general conclusion: "You can't hire anybody to do an honest day's work." "Coffee doesn't have any strength any more." "I see they've indicted another cop. They ought to clean up the department." Since hasty conclusions form the unsound premises on which you are daily asked to act, you can keep out of much trouble by asking: "Are we sure that is true? Have we enough examples? Have we checked enough people's opinions? Have we run enough tests to be sure? Is this merely a matter of opinion from which no dependable conclusion can be drawn?"

While it is easy to spot a hasty generalization, it is not always easy to say when you have studied enough instances to justify a decision. Here is a point at which the distinction between the wise and the foolish, the amateur and the professional, the timid and the confident, the dull and the imaginative becomes clear.

2. The second trap makes these distinctions even more acute. The question here is not, "How many instances have you observed?" but, "Have you observed appropriate instances under proper conditions?"

If, for instance, you accepted the invitation above to agree that Mrs. Stiles was justified in deciding to trade at the Bumble Bee because its prices are lower than those of the other two markets, you overlooked the fact that such a decision should involve the quality of the food as well as the price. Are you sure that the food at the Bumble Bee is not inferior to that of the other markets? Are you sure that Mrs. Stiles bought in each store the same objects so that her comparisons made sense? Are you sure that Mrs. Stiles did not go to the Bumble Bee only on sales days? What other shops might she trade at?

To be the basis for a valid conclusion, your instances should be representative and not exceptional, and they should be observed under conditions that permit correct interpretation.

The combination of *induction and deduction* is inevitable in the solution of most difficult problems. Difficult problems involve sub-problems. Each of these has to be decided in accordance with its own circumstances and by its own appropriate logical steps.

Sam Richmond is just completing his Senior year in law school. He has to decide whether to return home to Hazelton, N.C., to practice or to enter a firm in New York. As you turn this problem over in your own mind, you can see how many separate though related problems Sam has to solve. Let's take one or two.

The key question seems to Sam to be, "Do I prefer the greater opportunities of a New York firm or the greater independence of Hazelton?" Buried in that choice is the generalization that there are more opportunities for a lawyer in New York than in a southern town. Sam has talked to enough lawyers in both places to know that, if he measures the word "opportunities" by the two yardsticks of income and importance of cases, the generalization is justified. But another opportunity also interests Sam. He would like to be a leader in his community and perhaps enter politics. Hazelton seems to offer better opportunities for him in this direction. He knows personally that most lawyers in Hazelton are community leaders and a number are prominent in local and state politics. Here Sam's approach is primarily inductive. By examining individual instances, he establishes his own major premise—Hazelton lawyers have an excellent opportunity to become community leaders and to enter politics. Then he applies it deductively to himself—"If I become a lawyer in Hazelton, I shall have an excellent opportunity to do the same." You realize, of course, that Sam is not working out a true syllogism, for the terms "excellent opportunity" do not signify inevitability. No matter how favorable the conditions for lawyers in general, if Sam has certain personal disqualifications—a police record, say—the generalization will not apply to him. But Sam has silently accepted another major premise: "All Hazelton lawyers with my social and personal qualifications share whatever opportunities are open to Hazelton lawyers."

In a whole series of steps, some of them examined carefully and consciously, others accepted consciously but without examination, and yet others accepted unconsciously, Sam finally makes his decision. Reasoning about problems combines building up generalizations from instances and applying generalizations to instances in kaleidoscopic mixture. To make logic work for you in problem solving, you have to keep a sharp eye on this blending of induction and deduction.

Your awareness of how logic enters into problem solving will help keep you alert not only to reject an unjustified inference but also to determine at what point an inference is sufficiently valid to be acted on. Here is where you have to take leave of formal logic and cultivate what you might call logical-mindedness. For in estimating the probability of success or failure in a course of action, you will usually make your decision on the basis of inferences not valid in formal logic. We shall pursue the determination of probability in the next chapters on analogy and cause and effect.

•   •   •

Analyze some of your past problems until you know when you are reasoning deductively, when inductively, and when by a combination of the two. . . . Study the errors in deduction illustrated by the examples of the snakes and the mushrooms. Find illustrations of these errors in your own problems. . . . Select three of your recent problems where you came to a conclusion from a number of instances.

How many instances did you employ in each case? Have your conclusions proved correct? . . . In a current problem that is bothering you, see if you can find (1) any hasty generalizations, (2) any generalizations based on inappropriate instances or conditions. . . . Do you think you can increase your logical-mindedness? How?

18

Analogy

❧ *A few fossilized bones* ❧

IN OSHKOSH, Wisconsin, the police caught a burglar who had been having phenomenal success in discovering hidden cash in the houses he robbed. "Easy," he explained, "I just watched my wife hide ours." He was using analogy—one of the commonest, most trusted, and least trustworthy means of problem solving that man has yet thought up. Yet it is part of scientific reasoning, too. Therefore you need to know when you can rely on inferences drawn from analogies and when you cannot.

Let us say that last year you met the problem of a seasonal slump in sales by increased advertising, with satisfactory results. You reason that if you use the same solution in a similar problem this year, you will get satisfactory results again. This is problem solving by analogy.

It is easy to see why this method is common and trusted. Essentially, it is the method we all use to assimilate experience. In day-by-day living over the years you have to accept analogy—the likeness between two situations—as a guide to solving recurrent problems. But you see in the sales problem why analogy is untrustworthy. Maybe last year buyers had more money. Maybe this year your competitors are much more active. Maybe this year you will have to advertise on television at a much higher cost. Maybe the same sort of solution for the same sort of problem will work; maybe it will not.

When is likeness between two problems the basis for certainty

141

that they can be solved in the same way? The answer is: Only when the likeness is 100 per cent complete. You can reliably assume that you can hard-boil a fresh egg by keeping it submerged in boiling water for ten minutes. The likeness between any two fresh hens' eggs and the likeness between any two pans of boiling water make this probability, for all practical purposes, a certainty. Millions of tests have reduced this problem to a simple application of deductive reasoning.

At this level you are using analogy as a matter of simple *correspondence.* You are saying: "A is like B. What is true of B is true of A." As you saw in the previous chapter on logic, this kind of reasoning has certainty only when A and B correspond to the extent of sharing exactly the characteristics of a class—as two fresh hens' eggs do.

Analogy, then, is basic to the operation of induction and deduction. The instances originally tested to build up a general truth inductively must first be selected according to their likenesses. And the truth of a deductive syllogism cannot be applied to a single instance until its likeness to other members of the class of objects covered has been established.

If this simplification does not make things simple for you, keep going as though nothing had happened. Analogy is used so universally as a problem-solving device that it is imperative to show how restricted its reliability is and yet how valuable it can be.

Problems in which conditions correspond exactly to those of past problems are like hard-boiling an egg. They are routine affairs. Your real task is to figure out how to use analogy when the matching up is not perfect. Then your effort to approach your problems in a scientific spirit forces you to calculate much more warily the reliability of inferences drawn from similarities.

How do you do this? By pressing for the answer to one question: Is the correspondence precise enough to be applicable in this problem? You cannot accept without scrutiny the inference that if A and

B are alike in some respects—perhaps in many—they are alike in the manner and degree necessary for use in a certain situation. The brothers Jim and Joe are identical twins. The extent of the likeness— similarities of looks, voice, and personality traits—may be sufficient for a sales job but meaningless if you want to hire Jim to repair television sets, and he is not trained in that craft. Neil, who is not at all like Joe in any other respect, is a better answer if he is, like Joe, a skilled television repairman. Because Muggins, the family dog, is harmless, his small master thinks the mad dog he meets on the street is harmless. If a horse wins one race, the unwary bet their pay checks on the likelihood of his winning the next one. Trying to solve one specialized problem on the basis of one other experience is dubious business. Reasoning from the particular to the particular is the most primitive form there is.

Now let's consider analogy as you use it beyond the level of simple correspondence—as the term is strictly used in logic and science.

You use analogy more creatively when it involves a carry-over from one situation to an essentially different one with some elements in common. For instance, you might speculate: "Blueberries are known to require two or more bushes to pollinate successfully. Perhaps my apple tree isn't bearing because I have only one." An analogy of this sort suggests what may prove a useful approach to a problem. It offers no inevitable correlation. What is true of blueberry bushes may be true of apple trees. You make no assumption that it must be true.

Analogy suggests rather than proves. You will find analogy is most fruitful as a means of suggesting a hypothesis, to be tested in the usual ways. A zoologist, seeing a few fossilized bones which resemble those of a horse, though smaller and differing in certain respects, develops a concept of what the forerunner of the horse looked like in, say, the Miocene age. A zoologist's knowledge of the anatomy of a horse enables him to see likenesses that you and I might miss. An anthropologist observing the marriage customs of a tribe in central

143

Africa develops a clearer concept of marriage in America. Analogies suggest applications to minds that are prepared to take the cue.

Here is one of the ways you might use analogy to attack one of your problems. You manufacture Symo, a medical oil. One of the ingredients, Gamma, becomes scarce and expensive. It is derived from a Mexican plant. Your search to find a substitute starts with your collecting all American plants with similar characteristics— say the presence of chemical compound Psi. Your hypothesis is that the most logical place to find a substitute for Gamma is in an analogous source. This inference is reasonable. It has a higher probability rating than any other hypothesis you can advance. But you know that it is not certain. Ultimately you may find a better source of Gamma in a mineral, or you may restructure your problem and manufacture your product without Gamma.

Nevertheless, you proceed on the course with the highest probability of success. Your research on American plants extends your use of analogy. Now it is a more exact scientific process. You may conduct hundreds of experiments over a long period before you find— or are convinced that you cannot find—an American plant from which a substitute can be got satisfactorily. "Satisfactorily" means that it will match the Gamma you are using in all its chemical properties and will at least approach it in availability and cost of production. To come to a decision, you may have to make comparisons of extraordinary exactness and number. Analogy has determined your approach, analogy has guided you on your way, and analogy has ruled your decision.

As indicated in the chapter on experiment, sampling is a basic technique for problem solving by analogy. If you want to know what kind of corn you are buying, you strip back the husks of an ear or two at random. If you wish to know what people think about garbage removal service in your city, you call up ten or twenty housewives. The validity of the process rests on the degree of likeness between the

144

ones you chance to select and all of the others. You should not have much trouble judging the reliability of such sampling.

But suppose that the problem is one of inventory control in the Symo oil products industry. You have to estimate what is the most efficient amount of raw materials and finished products to have on hand. Since this problem is shot through with the variables that affect sources of supply, transportation, space, labor, and sales, obviously any ordinary system of sampling will be useless. Only extensive data subjected to rigorous mathematical treatment—including allowances for error—can make your sampling usable. (The Census of the United States is taken this way. It is more accurate than the census takers' actual figures.) Still, your underlying reasoning is that what is true of a representative sample or cross section is true of the whole because you have contrived to make it scientifically resemble all the other parts.

In a problem of moderate complexity you are likely to make use of analogy in one of two ways. For instance, to determine what is probably true about a whole organization or system of some kind, you study intensively either *one unit* or *one phase*. To make a study of the effectiveness of the sales techniques in a chain of markets, you might analyze all the selling done by one typical market—one unit of the chain. Or you might analyze one phase of the selling—the selling in one department or the selling of one item—throughout the entire chain. In the first method you are saying that what is true of all phases of one typical unit in a system is probably true of all other typical units in the system. In the second method you are saying that what is true about one phase in all units of a system is probably true about all phases of the system. Use of both methods will of course offset to some extent the errors in either. To give such methods any predictability value, however, you would have to keep regular records of your comparisons. But once you have established trustworthy records of parallel experiences in the past, you have a useful, if not infallible, tool for working on the problems of the present and future.

The historical approach is another type of problem solving from hypotheses suggested by analogy.

Is war with Russia inevitable? To answer this question the historian Arnold Toynbee points out that after the Crimean War, in which the Western Powers defeated Russia, Russia tried to reverse its defeat by expanding eastward. Twice, in 1878 and in 1885, Great Britain was on the verge of going to war with Russia. Yet within twenty-two years the two nations entered into an entente with one another to face the mutual menace of Germany. Twice, in 1914 and in 1941, they went to war against Germany as allies.

Both the usefulness and the naked weakness of analogy are clear in this example. Is war with Russia inevitable? No, says Toynbee, because in the past when it looked inevitable, war with Russia did not take place. Instead, in two wars she became the ally of the country it seemed she was going to fight. This historical observation answers the literal point of the question. We cannot accept the certainty of war with Russia, for in equally threatening circumstances it has been avoided in the past. That is reassuring. But it does not prove anything. All of the circumstances have changed—the actors, the grievances, the strength of the various world powers, the aims of the Russian rulers. Reduced to its genuine limits, Toynbee's analogy is only mildly relevant. To argue that because the Russians did not go to war in similar circumstances in the past, they will not in the future is invalid. There is no certain relationship between the past and the present or future.

Yet with all its hazards analogy is a valuable tool for solving problems. If you are a lawyer, the whole structure of precedents on which you base your cases and on which courts decide them rests on the reasoning that what was upheld as true in precedent A should be accepted as true of B, which closely resembles A. No scientific exactness of resemblance is involved here. No experimental tests can prove the similarity is exact and relevant. Only your shrewd analysis can make the similarity plausible, and only judicial wisdom can determine the degree of applicability. Yet the decision must be rendered —the legal problem solved.

Sometimes what makes a problem difficult is the lack of apparent likeness to any other problem. Before you can bring your experience to bear on a problem, you must find points of resemblance to past problems and solutions. Sometimes in an analogous situation, dissimilar conditions exist. Then it is up to you to find the variable, in order to prevent acting as though the conditions were identical. Both of these situations challenge you as a problem solver. Here is where education and wide experience contribute to imaginative problem solving. They increase the number of analogues from which you can draw connections and make inferences other people miss. As Francis Bacon said long ago, the good problem solver must have "a mind nimble and versatile enough to catch the resemblances of things, and at the same time steady enough to fix and distinguish their differences."

• • •

How many times during the past twenty-four hours have you made fairly important decisions on the basis of analogy? How logical have you been? . . . Pick out a problem in which your use of analogy seems critical. What exactly is your reasoning? What is A and what is B? Are they specifics, like individual people or solutions? Or are they general, like groups of people or kinds of procedure? Or is the A of your problem a specific being compared with B, a general—as an individual person with a group? Now you are ready to ask your two key questions: (1) What is the extent of the similarity? and (2) What kind of likeness exists? In the light of the discussion in this chapter, how does your use of analogy stand up? Do you think it is scientifically sound? Reasonably dependable? Dubious? . . . Do you see that the validity of your reasoning depends on how close you can come to establishing a syllogism—that is, to proving that A is in all relevant respects identical with B, which is either a group that without exception performs in a certain way, or which is a typical member of such a group? If you are carrying on an experimental approach, the representative nature of the samples you use requires your special scrutiny. . . . If you have a problem where you are using analogy but cannot establish a scientific correspondence, the usefulness of your method will depend on the probability you derive from the extent and relevance of the analogy. . . . If you have a perplexing problem before you in which you are not using analogy to arrive at your conclusions, you might search for one to suggest a hypothesis by which you can attack your problem.

19

Cause and Effect

❧ *Some fancy billiards* ❧

When Columbus was marooned on the north shore of Jamaica in 1508, writes Samuel E. Morison in the *Admiral of the Ocean Sea*, he faced one of the most difficult problems of his troubled career. The Admiral and four hundred and fifty men were totally dependent upon the natives for food. Then the natives, tired of accumulating trinkets, ceased to aid the Spaniards. How could they be induced to resume?

Columbus consulted the prediction of eclipses in an almanac he had brought with him. A few days later, he threatened the natives that God would send that very night a token of his wrath for their neglect. When an eclipse occurred on schedule, the terrified natives came running with provisions.

In solving his problem, Columbus used cause and effect. To get the desired effect—help from the natives—he had to set in motion a cause that would produce that effect. Actually he started a chain reaction. The eclipse produced fear, fear produced a cooperative attitude, and that induced the natives to resume bringing food. On the other hand, the natives made an unjustified inference when they thought that Columbus caused the eclipse.

The enormous importance of cause and effect in the scientific approach to problem solving and the hazards that go with its use make it worth thorough consideration.

149

Let's take a well-known social problem—mental disease in the United States. As you know, the number of inmates in our mental hospitals has increased tremendously in recent years. You will agree with most people, I imagine, that mental disease is increasing. But according to some authorities you are drawing the wrong conclusion. They say that there is increasing knowledge of mental troubles among doctors and laymen, and there are more and better facilities being built to take care of mental cases. They say that these factors cause an increase in the number of inmates of institutions. But they maintain that there has been no provable increase in mental disease itself.

You see that cause and effect are tricky customers. But before we grapple with the trickiness of cause and effect or try to figure out how to use them, let's try to say simply what we are talking about.

In trying to solve a problem by reasoning from cause to effect, you say, "This cause (or these causes) will produce this effect." In reasoning the other way, you say, "This effect was produced by this cause (or these causes)." This is wonderfully simple. Yet it is the heart of the business.

Solving problems by working from cause to effect is always working into the future. Every time you wonder, "What would happen if . . . ?", you are thinking from cause to effect.

When it became necessary to fence in the cattle on the western prairies, wooden rails and boards were out of the question because of expense. The cattle leaned against wire and broke it down. Still, wire had to be the answer. The problem then was to find a cause that would produce the desired effect, an economical wire fence that cattle would not knock down. An Illinois farmer named Glidden wondered what would discourage cattle from leaning on fences; he invented barbed wire. Now a light charge of electricity in a single strand of wire gets the same results.

Working from effect to cause is always working backwards in time. Every time you ask, "Why did this happen?", you are thinking from effect to cause. Every whodunit is an exercise in problem solving

150

from effect to cause. All trouble shooting in industry follows this procedure.

By going back to the examples of Christopher Columbus and of mental illness, you will note at once that we do not always employ this cause and effect technique in a simple one-step arrangement. Sometimes we do. But you can see from these two cases that some fancy billiards can be involved.

Yet the cause to effect technique is straightforward enough. Columbus figured, "If I can only scare these superstitious natives into believing that I have supernatural powers, they will consider it advisable to bring us food." The prophecy followed by the eclipse was the cause that yielded the desired effect.

In a difficult problem we are more likely to be trying to find the cause for an effect in order to change the effect by changing the cause.

How's that again?

Suppose one of the tires on your car is soft. That condition is probably the effect of a slow leak. You set to work to find the cause, presumably a puncture, not as an end in itself but so that you can stop it up and prevent your tire from going soft again.

Much of the time, therefore, you work backwards from an effect to its cause in order to work forward from cause to effect again. You might want to secure a new, better effect. Or you might want to apply the same cause to secure a similar effect in another situation.

Now it becomes clear indeed that the whole usefulness of cause and effect as a means of solving problems depends on three conditions: (1) Whether or not the causal relationship that you say exists does in fact exist; (2) whether or not it is the only one that exists; and (3) whether or not it exists with the inevitability that you assert. Since all problem solving is as peppered with causal relations as a watermelon is with seeds, you simply must get a firm hold on these three "whethers." Let's see how they work.

1. It is natural to assume that an increase in the number of inmates

in mental hospitals is caused by an increase in mental disease. But other not-so-obvious causes actually bring about this increase. The inferred relationship does not exist.

2. Almost any one of us asked to name the causes of the British defeat in the Revolutionary War probably would come up with a standard eighth-grade answer about the superior fighting qualities of the colonists and the superior leadership of General Washington. These are causes but not the only causes. Most of us would fail to assign as one major cause Britain's loss of control of the sea when three of the greatest navies in the world—those of France, Spain, and Holland—joined the colonies. The inferred relationship is not the only one.

3. When Columbus invented his deception, he could only hope it would produce the effect he desired. The eclipse might not have scared the natives, or it might have scared them away entirely. Few human responses are scientifically predictable. The inferred relationship is not inevitable.

As you think over these three cases, you will see that the *inevitability* of the causal relationship with which you are dealing is the crux of its value in problem solving. You cannot accept as probable a causal relationship in a problem you are trying to solve until you have proved that (1) it does in fact exist, (2) it cannot be attributed to other causes or produce other effects, (3) it must take place or have taken place as you indicate.

Your neighbor's son Donald asks you to help him solve the problem: Should he join a fraternity? "Yes, he should," says his cousin Bob. "Statistics prove that more fraternity men than nonfraternity men become top executives. Therefore, fraternities help men succeed after college." Since there are many more nonfraternity men, even among college graduates, than fraternity men, cousin Bob is probably rolling his own statistics. But for the sake of trying to help Donald solve his problem, you accept for the moment the premise that among executives the percentage of fraternity men is higher than that of

152

nonfraternity men. Bob's argument must be that membership in a fraternity is the cause of this success. Since he says nothing about any other cause, the inference is that fraternity membership is the sole cause. Obviously, this is nonsense. The charitable interpretation is that Bob means that fraternity membership is a significant factor in the success of those executives who were fraternity men in college. And, further, of course, he is saying to Donald that therefore being a fraternity man will be of significant help to him in his future.

Bob's contribution is little help in solving Donald's problem. The cause and effect relationship will not stand up. (1) Why is it that the cause and effect relationship does not apply to the large number of fraternity men who do not become successful executives? (2) Is it not probable that other causes are more important—the possibility that boys with the talent to run organizations join organizations in college, or that many fraternity men come from families with established business connections? (3) What reason is there to think that the factors that might aid Donald in becoming an executive would have the same effect if he were to become a doctor or a musician? Do you recognize that these are the same three tests we just discussed in the previous paragraphs?

You see that the usefulness of cause and effect is severely limited if the cause you are working with might produce other effects or if the effect you start with might have resulted from causes other than the one you ascribe. The factors that keep a cause-and-effect relation from being inevitable and foolproof are called variables. These are the jokers you will have to keep your eye on. Watch for the variables.

Let us take an everyday problem and imagine how you would handle the causal relations.

A series of car accidents proves that a certain street intersection in your town is dangerous. You are assigned the task of recommending appropriate action. You adopt the hypothesis that the unusual number of accidents at this one spot must be the effect of special causes. You inspect the location. It looks like this: Sycamore is the main

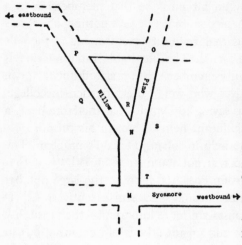

street of the town. Because of hills and a river, the only direct route through town is along Willow and Sycamore. The dangerous intersection is N. Triangle *PON* is a small one—no more than two or three houses on a side. There is a stop sign at N but no light. There are traffic lights at intersections *P, O,* and *M.* A bus station is at *Q,* a filling station at *R,* and a taxi office at *S.*

You observe what happens. A car coming along Pine comes to a full stop at N. With a green light at M it edges out but often cannot nose into the heavy traffic on Willow before the light changes, and the Willow line piles up solid. The car from Pine is then caught broadside in the left lane of Willow as the traffic from Sycamore sweeps around the corner building, *T.* You conclude that the lack of a light at N, the heavy through traffic, the large number of interstate trucks and buses, the high percentage of out-of-town drivers, the nearly blind turn from Sycamore into Willow, and the extra congestion about the bus station, filling station, and taxi office are the special causes of the problem.

Can you remove any of these causes? After consideration, you say no. Your first thought is to place a traffic light at intersection N. This action would bring about undesirable effects. The distance between N and M is only about fifteen yards. Two lights so close together would jam up the through traffic. Strangers coming around the blind corner would be ambushed if they ran into a red light immediately. Staggering the three lines of traffic would be possible but complicated.

What other courses are open? How else can you get the effect you want? What, by the way, is that? Is it to create a safe intersection at N? Not necessarily. Your real problem is to stop the accidents. Can you cause N not to be an intersection? How? Can you do it by means of a one-way street formula? You try out this hypothesis. It works. By making Pine Street one-way eastbound from N to O, and Willow Street one-way westbound from P to N, you can have the three lines of traffic, controlled by lights, safely flow around the triangle without crossing one another. You have achieved the primary effect you want, safety, and also a secondary one of making the stretch by the bus station much more convenient for everyone.

In solving this problem you followed the familiar pattern mentioned earlier. You started with an effect. You determined its causes. You used these causes to guide you in setting new causes in motion to achieve a new effect, more desirable than the original one.

In cause-and-effect relationships, as in all other phases of problem solving, your sharpest challenge comes when the interaction of factors is most obscure. Then you are forced to unobvious answers.

Sometimes you may aim at producing one general condition as the effect of a number of causes. Influencing public opinion follows this pattern. Sometimes the solution of a relatively small problem holds in it the solution of much larger ones. When Charles F. Kettering invented the electric self-starter, he had in mind a result larger than the mechanical one he achieved. He was interested in increasing the use of automobiles in America. He accomplished this larger end. The sale of cars zoomed because for the first time women could drive them with ease.

Problems often go half solved until hidden causes are uncovered. Then better results are possible because fresh answers are possible. For instance, fatigue among industrial workers seems so natural that the obvious answer is to see that they are not required to work too hard. But John U. Grimaldi of the Association of Casualty and Surety Companies recently told the Society of Mechanical Engineers that fatigue in modern industry is not caused by hard physical exertion but by psychological factors. He outlined eight ways to reduce fatigue among industrial workers: (1) Engineering the job to produce maximum efficiency through better illumination, ventilation, posture, motion study, safety and health provisions, noise control, and plant orderliness; (2) selective placement of employees on proper jobs; (3) lessening of friction by sound human relations; (4) speeding up production lines only after full consideration of effect on the worker; (5) avoidance of work week beyond forty-eight hours, if possible; (6) five-minute rest each hour in monotonous work; (7) rotating shifts every two or three months instead of weekly; (8) educational programs to teach good posture, hygiene, nutrition, recreation, relaxation.

You will stumble over one fallacy connected with cause and effect so many times that you should now give it your close attention. Here is how it works:

For many years doctors observed a much higher incidence of cirrhosis of the liver among alcoholics than among members of any other group. There was no reason to doubt that excessive consumption of alcohol caused the disease. Now it is known that the cause of cirrhosis of the liver is not alcohol but vitamin deficiency. Lack of vitamins comes from lack of food. If an alcoholic ate properly, he would not get cirrhosis of the liver. Any teetotaler can get the disease from a vitamin deficiency.

Go back to the example of the mental hospitals at the beginning of the chapter. We observe an increase in patients in mental hospitals, and we incorrectly infer an increase in the incidence of mental disease—that is, that in every 1000 people there are now more suffering from mental disorders than there were fifty years ago. We have mistaken a close relationship for a causal one, just as in the

156

alcohol-cirrhosis of the liver association. We have in effect reasoned that because night follows day, day causes night. This fallacy has the classic tag, *Post hoc ergo propter hoc*—"After this, therefore because of this."

This variant of cause and effect is sometimes called inference from sign. Wrapped up in the cirrhosis problem you can see the usefulness of reasoning from sign as well as its weakness. While doctors were wrong to infer that heavy drinking caused the disease, they were right in inferring a significant connection. They still have three well-tested hypotheses to work with: (1) This sick alcoholic may have cirrhosis of the liver. (2) If this alcoholic does not give up drinking, he may get this disease. (3) If this alcoholic, who has cirrhosis of the liver, gives up drinking, he may eat regularly and his health may improve.

You will find one of the most interesting ways of solving your problems is by means of clues or signs. Here is an example. The tomato plants in your garden do not yield tomatoes. That effect may be produced by a number of causes. You consult an expert. He asks, "Did the leaves turn yellow?" You say they did. "Then," he says, "your plants are probably not getting enough nitrogen. Fertilizer should help them." You fertilize them, and they begin to yield.

The yellow leaves are only a minor part of the whole effect of the lack of nitrogen. But to the experienced gardener they are a reliable —though not infallible—sign of the cause of the trouble. Once the cause is suspected, you at least have a hypothesis to work on. When you think about this procedure for a while, you will see that essentially you are betting on *association*. While the leaves of tomato plants may turn yellow from other causes, the experienced gardener associates this effect with lack of nitrogen.

When a doctor decides that a patient may have a certain disease because of the presence of symptoms usually associated with that disease, he is using signs to guide him. If the symptoms are associated only with that disease, then the inference has a high degree of certainty. But the infinite complexity of the human system and the multiplicity of its ailments make the exact reading of symptoms a subtle art. The expert diagnostician is the doctors' doctor, for he helps solve their most difficult problems.

In the intersection problem you dealt with straightforward cause and effect relationships: What makes this intersection dangerous? What can be done to remove the danger? The nature of the trouble is clear, the causes are not hard to discover, and the means to secure better results emerge after study. But the kind of clues that lead to the correct diagnosis of complex problems—the forecast of financial conditions in a certain industry, say—are, like the symptoms in many illnesses, not at all easy to detect or to add up correctly.

When Columbus on his first voyage met birds flying and a branch of an unfamiliar species of bush with berries and a pole carved with tools drifting in the sea, he concluded that he was nearing land with human inhabitants. These objects are consistently associated with inhabited land, and no other explanation is plausible. What you search for, then, are these clues, signs, minor effects, or whatever you care to call them that you know do have a high consistency of association or can be proved to have.

Certain diseases occur in a high percentage of cases in both identical twins when one is affected. This correlation—this high consistency of relationship between the affliction of both twins and the affliction of one—is a valid basis for inferring that heredity plays a part in these diseases. In forecasting the financial outlook of a certain industry, you might base your predictions on signs such as carloadings, output of the steel industry, building construction, or population shifts. Your experience leads you to accept a reasonably reliable correlation between these activities and the prosperity of your industry. The reliability would not be nearly as high as in the case of certain diseases of twins.

In human relations inference from sign has a poor record. Yet the process goes on all the time, and we decide some of our most im-

158

portant problems by beliefs and prejudices based on its dubious aid. Leadership in our society has been badly confused because so many people insist on following the superficial signs of leadership rather than the proved evidence of it. We take the bustling manner, the commanding voice, the shrewd silence, or other trappings of leadership as evidence that the possessor of these traits has the other requirements. A baffled college trustee once said when asked why he had helped appoint a bumbling president, "Damn it, he looks like a college president!"

Inference from sign, like inference from analogy, is useful to you for the hypotheses it suggests. It helps you to find out what might have happened in the past or to decide what might happen in the future. Your experience and your imagination can to a large degree be measured by your skill in perceiving significant clues and in making useful inferences from them.

You will find the complexity and uncertainty of the variables involved make cause and effect always a troublesome part of your problems. No aspect of problem solving will make greater demands on you. None is closer to the heart of the scientific approach.

• • •

Since your reasoning about cause and effect tends to have a crucial bearing on your problem solving, here is an opportunity to criticize your practice. . . . First select one past problem where you have based your solution largely on cause-to-effect reasoning. Did the effect follow as you predicted? If not, should you have foreseen why it would not? Now do the same thing with a problem where you reasoned from effect back to cause. In either case were you more concerned with immediate causes and effects or with secondary ones? . . . Now you are ready to trace your cause and effect reasoning in a difficult current problem. Where have you reasoned that certain causes would probably bring about certain effects? Where have you reasoned that certain effects probably were brought about by certain causes? Examine each one in detail. To each one apply the three test questions: (1) Does the causal relationship that you say exists in fact exist? (2) Does it exist in the degree that you assert? (3) Does it exist with the inevitability that you believe? Take the negative side and try to throw doubt on the degree of probability involved in each causal relation by applying the same three tests. Try to prove that one or more of the three fallacies are present—(1) a certain effect cannot come solely from the cause chosen; (2) the apparent cause is not the true cause; (3) an association has been mistaken for a causal relation. How well does your reasoning survive this two-way check? . . . Can you discover any instances where you have made inferences from signs? Have they been valid? Imaginative? Fallacious?

Part IV

ART

IN THIS final section you think about three large aspects of problem solving. Just as reason underlies all methods of diagnosis and attack, so behind all the same efforts stand *Experience* and *Imagination*. In these two chapters you see how they operate and how you might apply them more effectively. Your experience and your imagination combine to enable you to reach solutions without depending on reason alone. Then to clinch the idea that you cannot reduce problem solving to mechanical procedures, you are encouraged to look at it as having always the characteristics of a *Calculated Risk*. These three aspects add another dimension to problem solving. They make it an art.

20

Experience

"I F HISTORY teaches anything," some cynic has said, "it is that we invariably disregard what it has to teach." Aristotle says something like, "The way to learn to play a harp is to play it—and that is also the way to learn to play it badly." And Fritz Roethlisberger of the Harvard Graduate School of Business Administration says, "The school of hard knocks makes criminals as well as businessmen."

These firecrackers are meant to wake you up so that you will not trip over any old saws about experience. Experience *is* the best teacher. But it does not necessarily teach you the best answers to your problems or the quickest way to solve them. Common-sense judgments based on the daily experiences of one person are often much too limited to be applied to new problems.

But having sounded this warning, let us admit the importance of experience in the art of problem solving. Where science and reason leave off and art and inspiration begin is largely a question of terminology. We grant that the successful application of scientific methods to a problem is itself an art, and we grant that in every difficult problem the rational techniques are supplemented by nonrational insights. In your approach to every problem and in your final decision about it, you rely on both reason and inspiration. For our purpose the aspects of problem solving that make it an art are mainly experi-

163

ence, imagination, intuition, and that flexibility that sees each problem as a calculated risk.

In a limited sense, the experienced man is a man who has faced problems similar to the one that confronts him at a particular time and has developed methods for handling them. Experience provides a Pullman porter with a skill in making an upper berth that cannot be matched by the brains and experience of bank presidents, atomic scientists, or chess champions. Only nurses, hotel maids, and old soldiers—people with similar experience—can match him.

The other day I watched two strong workmen trying to pull a twelve-foot pipe out of the ground. They had a rope twisted around it, and they hauled this way and that to loosen it. They strained till they were purple as they raised it a tiny bit at a time. A high school boy, who had none of their experience in such matters but who had remembered some of the things he had studied, suggested that they put a car jack into a loop in the rope, rest the jack on a timber, and then apply this leverage. The men did and the pipe came out with little trouble.

Both of these workmen were familiar with jacks and the principle of leverage. They simply forgot to use what they knew because they associated jacks only with cars and buildings. The boy with little practical experience and only a smattering of school physics, looked at the men struggling with their problem and then canvassed his meager resources to see what he did know that might apply. He used his experience but in a broader sense.

Experience is memory. As you size up a problem, experience puts into the equation factors that are familiar. In algebra or chemistry, these are the knowns. Only through the manipulation of knowns can you determine the unknowns and manipulate them. A garage mechanic sets about repairing a foreign car he has never seen before by finding out what parts are like those in American cars. Then his knowledge of motors enables him to identify the function of other parts. Knowledge of their function aids him to understand their operation. Then he can find the trouble and make his repairs.

Recognition of the familiar in a problem may give you a clue to a solution, no matter how intimidating the problem is. Do you not remember how you would sit petrified before an arithmetic problem when you were a child and then discover with delight that some features of it you had met and conquered before?

You probably know a number of relatively uneducated men and women who run complicated activities and make fast decisions about the problems that face them. They have what we call know-how. Making a living from buying and selling fish or flowers may seem to you and me much too difficult to dream of undertaking. Yet many men and women whose only training is experience do make their livings in these ways. Their ability to make money from solving the problems of fish markets and florist shops derives from the way in which the repetitiousness of experience reduces their business to a pattern of problems and answers that they can draw on without really going through the processes that would be forced on us. In a majority of cases they learned their trade as apprentices, by one of the most valuable forms of experience—imitation.

The value to an organization of many of its employees is largely their experience in that organization. Each organization has its own unwritten laws, its own practices, its own bagful of information, and its own cast of characters. No employee can be effective until he has learned how to use these special factors in solving the problems of the organization. Thus the year or two of training that a college graduate receives in industry is largely devoted to what to the young man seems like the unprofitable business of merely getting acquainted with procedures and people.

People are experience, too. "It's not what you know; it's who you know" is often quoted by young people taking their first look at the problem of getting a job. What escapes them is the core of truth in this remark. Whom you know can make a vast difference on your problem-solving scorecard. When you call up a supplier about a shortage in a shipment, will you have to say: "Is this the Carco Supply Company? I want to speak to somebody about a shortage in a shipment—"? Or will you be able to say: "Hello, Frank. This is Jim. Say, there was a shortage in that last shipment—"?

Experience reduces many problems to custom. Custom is a potent force worthy of being consulted in working out your problems and is not to be ignored with impunity. Efficiency efforts aim largely at reducing mechanical operations to customary procedures that require little or no conscious thought. No one can drive a car in heavy traffic efficiently or operate a turret lathe efficiently or crochet efficiently who has to stop and think out each step. Under certain conditions and for certain personalities, the more nearly the human being approaches the machine in the unvarying nature of these habits, the happier and more productive he is. For other conditions and personalities, habitual activity of this nature leads to boredom, frustration, and lowered productivity.

Much of our experience is acceptance of the customs of our "tribes"—the folkways, Sumner called them, of the several groups in which we hold membership. When we think of this acceptance as a good thing, we talk about adjusting to society. People who do not make the necessary adjustments are queer, antisocial, criminal, insane, or whatever the rest of the group decides—or rather, whatever a particular group decides. Many of your problems in human relations are based on the experience of the group—on your understanding of group customs and values.

What's done and not done can have the force of a law or logical premise or scientific fact in many human problems. Custom can do much to hold together cities of people under a rain of bombs, or it can keep them stupidly starving themselves while they throw away the nutritive parts of the grain that is their main food. Custom can be the furrow from which springs the flower of civilization, law, and it can be the maggoty breeding ground of man's most beastly crime, genocide.

Experience to be applicable must tell you which elements of earlier successes and setbacks are applicable to a present problem. If, therefore, you are to profit in the future by your present experience, you must be studying and remembering the solutions of problems as you go along—what false notions you started with, what wrong turns you made, what delays and errors occurred, what approach cracked the most problems, who came up with the best solutions. So that you will not be dependent merely on years of experience, you should keep some sort of record. A problem and solution file with brief notes indicating the significant factors is desirable. Post-mortem sessions with associates help. Like an electronic "brain" you correct your performance by reviewing your experience—by "feedback."

Failure to solve problems is often failure to use available resources. Since you generally have more resources to help you with a given problem than you ever use, an inventory of what you have will save time and be reassuring. Mechanical devices, publications, money, people with experience, good will, time, health, courage—these and other assets often need only to be reviewed in relation to a specific problem to be useful. Perhaps the least used of resources is publications. The public libraries are vast problem-solving repositories. For a few cents the state and national governments provide technical information on everything under the sun. But you will find your greatest satisfaction comes from building up your own reference library. The experience of other people then becomes an extension of your own.

Time ripens the fruits of experience as it does apples and grapes. To apply your experience, you must allow time for the identical or nearly identical problem to recur—as it does in making berths or selling carnations. Or you might allow time to draw from the specific solutions of the problems you have met some generalizations that

167

you can apply to new problems—as the boy did in the pipe and jack example.

Winston Churchill has said, "Experience may be a bridle or a spur." Experience may be a bridle to check your problem-solving drive. A young actress may bring to a dramatic role a freshness and zest that a more experienced actress cannot summon. Experience may dim your realization of the uniqueness of every problem. Problems are never exactly duplicated. As Mary Follett says, "The X of one situation should always be X^1 in the next." The problem of selling carnations on Sunday, May 11, will not be the same on Sunday, May 18. One Sunday may be rainy, the other Mother's Day. Over and over engineers told Charles Kettering that now-familiar improvements in motorcar engines could not be made. Sometimes they insisted even after he made them. Their experience made their minds run one way, like mechanical toys. Experience, therefore, should be a process of unlearning as well as of learning.

Experience is a spiral. As a small child you were a selfish individualist. Then you learned the rudimentary differences between mine and thine. Your pre-school world was your family, with the approval and affection of your mother and father as an important force. Your world expanded in school to include the opinion of teachers and companions. At each step of the way what is learned as true at one level must be revalued at the next. Then what seems settled must be examined all over again at still the next level. Way down the line your dad is a big strong man who can throw a ball with tremendous force. When you are a teen-ager, worshipping Bob Lemon and Robin Roberts, Dad shrinks and his pitching efforts are ludicrous. Yet years later, as you play ball with your own son, you think how wise your father was to teach you to play games.

This spiraling from problems of one order of difficulty and complexity to another more difficult and more complex can be illustrated, of course, by reference to mathematics or any other subject. Arithmetic, algebra, plane geometry, solid geometry, trigonometry, and calculus—the solution of really difficult problems must be based on experience that has followed a similar progression. More and more experience without constant analysis and synthesis keeps you at the the teen-age level of problem solving.

If you are called on to solve many different kinds of problems, then, clearly, wide problem-solving experience is what you need. The reason that great athletes often make mediocre coaches and managers, distinguished scholars undistinguished university presidents, and crack salesmen cracked-up executives is that their early experience in solving certain kinds of problems successfully is too narrow to be transferable to the kinds that face them in their later positions. The shaping of experience into ever more powerful instruments for solving ever more difficult problems is the true function of education.

If you look on problem solving as an art, then experience must be a spur. The strength and assurance derived from grappling with reality spurs you on to put your powers to the trial of new problems, to devise new modes of attack, and to strive for the wisdom needed to see more clearly into the pattern of things. Then like Churchill himself you find your successes and failures a spur to do a better job next time.

• • •

Using your current problems as test cases, estimate the sufficiency of your experience to deal with the problems facing you. How trustworthy is your experience? Is it providing you with the precise information, confidence, and flexibility you need to take these recent problems in stride? Or does it provide you with rule-of-thumb solutions and the illusion that these problems hold no fresh challenge? Or is your experience inadequate in some respects? Is it a bridle or a spur? . . . How available is the experience that bears on these new problems? Is it all in your head, or can you draw on written records of your past successes and failures? To what extent are you calling on the experience of others as a natural, available extension of your own experience? What written resources are you drawing on? Does your mastery of these current problems suggest that your experience is enabling you to handle problems of increasing orders of complexity? . . . If your examination has disclosed any serious deficiencies, you have a new problem. What can you do about broadening your experience?— work at another job temporarily? cultivate certain people, perhaps by joining organizations? enroll for a course of study? read by yourself? travel? Draw up a list of reference books you should have (1) in your office, (2) in your home. This will take time, visits to a library, and advice from a librarian.

21

Imagination

"Birds don't stop for stations," observes a five-year-old, and you are startled by the ease with which children make themselves at home in the realm of imagination. Imagination is not the property of children and poets alone. It is a practical thing. "The difference between victory and defeat," said the military historian Clausewitz, "often hangs on the silken thread of imagination."

Frederic W. Goudy, one of the leading American type designers, once explained the designing of a new type face. He said, "I think of a letter and then mark around the thought." This is a good definition of an act of imagination, even if it is a joking one. It lays bare the truth that, easy as creativeness may be in its outward manifestations, it is still a mystery.

Creative problem solving is ultimately as much a mystery as any other art that depends on the action of the imagination. But once you have glimpsed the simplest of its operations and understand what takes place, perhaps you can follow some of the same steps in your efforts to deal creatively with your own problems.

After hearing a violin recital by Heifetz, a friend once said to me: "He makes you feel that you are hearing a piece of music for the first time. Heifetz does something slightly different—maybe he plays a little faster or a little slower, a little louder or a little softer. He

171

never does anything violently different. But the effect is different, original. He deviates from the norm."

Here is a definition of originality, oversimplified but provocative—deviation from the norm. The norm stands for regularity, the expected, the routine. The crude, the sensational, the bizarre represent an excessive break with what is normal and acceptable. The Heifetz secret is to move between these two levels—to get away from the norm, yet never so far as to cease to suggest it.

This formula for originality is practiced by every bridge player who tries to fool his opponents by making an orthodox play with an unorthodox card—by every pitcher who on the two-and-three count must throw a strike but tries to throw it in a manner the batter does not expect—by every woman who tries to buy a hat that is in the mode of the moment and yet different from every hat other women are wearing—by every industrial designer who creates the new car styles of the season.

Of course, the questions still unanswered are: How does the creative mind hit on the original solution? And how does he do it—as he often does—so fast? The sculpture of Michelangelo, the plays of Shakespeare, the quartets of Beethoven—all the greatest works of art leave us gasping in disbelief that human beings could create them at all, let alone in the relatively short time they usually took.

Clearly, you first have to have an excellent working knowledge of the norm in any field before you can control your deviation with the right skill. Failure to accept this hard truth will put you among the half-baked artists, crank inventors, political dreamers, and fakers in all fields who find it much easier to be different than to master the fundamentals from which they are deviating.

Then creative problem solving seems to occur when the problem is attacked without anxiety in a mood of eagerness, complete absorption, and forgetfulness of everything else. Solving takes place best when the problem is sealed off, when attention is focused, not drawn away in several directions. Complete absorption is fatiguing, but it turns work into play.

Jean Renoir tells unforgettably how his father, Pierre Auguste Renoir, would paint his masterpieces in the last years of his life. The artist was bedridden with rheumatism, and he suffered such intense pain that he could not sleep. But on a good morning he might decide to paint a certain tree near the house. He would be carried to the spot and propped up before his easel. The paint brush would be put in his crippled hand. At once the pain would be forgotten, and in his total absorption in the vision of the tree, he would sing and paint joyfully until, exhausted, he had to be carried back to his bed.

The act of imagination that solves a difficult problem—the bright idea, the brain storm, the inspiration—is a leap. It is like the jumping of an electric current. It is often a crossing over from one experience to another—from a familiar, unconnected experience to a problem in process of solution. The most famous example is Newton's fictitious observation of the fall of an apple.

Under everyday conditions your use of imagination in solving problems does not involve extraordinary leaps. The first step is to free yourself from the tyranny of the obvious—to be willing to deviate from the norm. Any problem that can be settled by an obvious solution is not much of a problem. Or to put it another way, an obvious solution that satisfies you raises questions about your standards. Many organizations operate at 50 per cent efficiency because of the dead weight of mediocrity that drags them down. Too many of their problems are settled by routine solutions. You do not have to have delusions of genius to withhold approval of even a good solution, whenever time permits an effort to work out a better one. The inventor Peter Cooper expressed the creed of the true problem solver when he said simply, "I was always planning and contriving, and was never satisfied unless I was doing something different, something that had never been done before." The habit of dissatisfaction with the obvious and mediocre is your first step in cultivating a fresh and original attack.

A creative mind can find scope for activity on any kind of problem. George Whalon, a college superintendent of buildings and grounds, was stuck for a while by the problem of what to do about many loads of furniture he had to install in barracks that were being used temporarily to house unmarried veterans. He did not have anything like the number of men required to lug the tables and chairs and dressers up the stairs of the numerous buildings. And the miscellaneous assortment of bunks and lockers was merely supplementary and would by no means go all around. He had no system for fair distribution.

Being used to solving his own problems, George Whalon called on his imagination instead of requesting a directive from above. Just at the end of the day he had a load of furniture deposited on the ground outside each barrack. Within hearing of the students his men announced that they would be back in the morning to distribute the loads. During the night there was much tugging and hauling and stealthy activity in the barracks. Cocking an ear but staying carefully out of sight, George chuckled merrily. The moving in was accomplished without his raising a finger, and the distribution was carried out by means satisfactory to both parties.

Sometimes the imaginative solution is the reverse of the orthodox —just the one that supposedly will not work. When Sir Hubert Murray became governor of Papua, he faced the problem of head hunting and other killings. Realizing that the natives were living in the Stone Age, he did not punish murderers. He had them accompany him on long trips around the island as he administered justice. The intelligent ones he sent back to their villages as constables. They made excellent law enforcers.

In the struggle to find the answer to a hard problem, do not be quick to cancel any solution because there is something wrong with it. Push it around. Explore it. It may be fundamentally right. Or it may give the clue to the right answer.

Back in the early 1920's Walter Chrysler stood on the edge of ruin as he was about to launch the Chrysler car. It had the first commercial high-compression engine and a new design that he hoped would revolutionize the automotive industry. But Chrysler needed credit from the bankers in order to go ahead with production. And the bankers would extend no more credit unless the car was selling. Chrysler had been counting on the showing his car would make at the New York Automobile Show to secure both sales and credit. Then the officers of the show ruled that the regulations forbade the showing of a car that was not in production.

Walter Chrysler did not give up in despair. He pushed his problem around. If he could not place his car on display at the Grand Central Palace where the show was held, would there be any point in showing it somewhere else in New York? Obviously not, since he was not interested in the general public but only in the professional motorcar people. But this apparently wrong answer gave him the right one. The men he wanted to see his new car were in the habit of staying at the Hotel Commodore near the Grand Central Palace. Walter Chrysler hired the lobby of the Commodore, his car made a deep impression on the industry, and bankers granted the $5-million credit he needed to start his corporation.

Acute and ever-present awareness of what needs solving is the motor that keeps your imagination running and makes it trip the alarm bell when the clue to the proper solution appears. Keep your unsolved riddles in the forefront of your mind. Then you are alert to see the connection between your problem and a new development— say a new technical discovery, a change of circumstances, or a re-arrangement of personalities. To restate an old saying, necessity— the heavy pressure of problem responsibility—puts the squeeze on your imagination. William Shakespeare shaped his peerless imagination through years of turning out plays for his stock company against hurried deadlines, and Johann Sebastian Bach wrote immortal music to fulfill an unrelenting Sunday schedule. On the other hand, modern management now recognizes the danger of allowing top executives to be too busy. Executives must have time and freedom of mind if they are to plan and to decide with imagination and far-sightedness. The Du Pont corporation has nine vice-presidents with no operational responsibilities. Their job is to think.

The imagination of a genius is directly related to the intensity and clarity and persistence with which his consciousness is filled with problems to be solved. Look through the *Notebooks* of Leonardo da Vinci to see how true this thought is. A Dutch spectacles-maker named Hans Lippershey accidentally discovered the telescope when he happened to look through two lenses he was holding. But it was the great Italian Galileo who knew what to do with it. Problem solvers on the order of Leonardo da Vinci and Galileo are men who first of all see the pattern of existence more comprehensively and more vividly than the rest of us do. They are therefore able to discern relevant relationships with a speed and sureness that amazes the world.

Your control over your imagination is limited. In its highest manifestations imagination is the inexplicable attribute of genius. You can do nothing about it at this level. At an ordinary level of achievement you will reach imaginative solutions to your problems in proportion to how much you know about them and how intense and prolonged your absorption in them is. The incalculable dollars-and-cents value of imagination makes its neglect by education and industry strange. Since 1936, however, several hundred General Electric engineers have developed their talents in GE Creative Engineering courses. They apply problem-solving techniques to real problems. They also stretch their imagination by exercises such as exploiting the strength in unpromising solutions.

Let us take a practical problem and see how your imagination might help you solve it. The problem situation is this: You are the head of Tekko, Inc., a small organization that provides an advisory service to industry. Besides four senior specialists, you have ten technical men and women on your staff. They are highly trained, hard to find, and well paid. You have a problem situation when you realize that the turnover among the junior members is higher than it should be and the morale lower.

A study of the situation uncovers this problem: For their training and experience, the ten junior staff members believe they do not have sufficient responsibility or prestige. They are loyal and hard working, as well as difficult to replace. You like them personally and count on them to take over the work of the senior members, including your own job, one of these days. What can you do?

Your dilemma is that you cannot see any way to help the younger staff members without damaging the morale of the four older ones. What are your alternatives? Your service is not extensive. Each of the senior men has primary responsibility for relations with a few companies. Each is able to handle these relations alone. To assign any of these companies to the younger members would reduce the responsibilities and prestige of the senior men unfairly. You have to consider their length of service and their morale. You do not wish to expand. Even if you did, you could not expand enough to take care of ten people. And you would soon have exactly the problem you now have, but magnified.

You go back over your problem. You analyze it more precisely. Does it contain a decisive factor? What is the cause of the dissatisfaction? It is not money. It is not really the work the ten men and women do. Even "prestige" distorts what they are after. What they want is more emotional satisfaction. Call it fun—the fun of sharing in the top operations of the firm, modest as they seem to you.

You now have restructured the problem. No longer are you asking yourself, "How can I keep these men and women without giving them work that I don't have to give them?" Nor are you asking, "How can I give them some of the work of the four senior members?" You are now asking, "How can I give these ten men and women a greater sense of satisfaction by sharing in all of the operations of the firm?" There seems no obvious way that you can do that. You cannot divide the responsibilities and leave the senior members unruffled. Or can you? The word was not "divide"; it was "share." But you can think of no orthodox solution.

Yet you have evolved a hypothesis based on sharing. How can it be pushed around and made to fit? You talk to the four senior men. They understand the problem, appreciate your intention of protecting them, and offer to share their liaison duties with their younger colleagues. The catch is that good management does not justify paying ten people to be assistants to four when the four do not need assistance. But you have made a little more progress. You now have a hypothesis and agreement in principle about its applicability.

You call a meeting of all fourteen staff members and discuss the problem frankly. The meeting helps. The junior members agree with your diagnosis and are enthusiastic about the general approach to a solution, though they make clear that they do not wish to intrude on the activities of the senior members. They offer several suggestions, but the meeting breaks up with no solution reached. Still, your progress continues. You know you have diagnosed your problem correctly, and you know you can count on cooperation from the entire staff. Yet you are baffled. You can see your objective—the senior members and the junior members somehow sharing the direct association with the companies using your service. But how can you bring that about without the inefficiency of paying two or three people to do one man's work? You hold your problem out before your mind's eye and scan it from all sides as you twirl it round and round.

Unbidden, at breakfast a new solution pops up instead of the toast you are waiting for. You will change the name of your firm from Tekko, Inc. to Tekko Associates. Each of the younger members of the staff will be invited as an associate to share with a senior member in all of the relations with two or three companies. He will go to meetings with the clients, take part freely in all planning, offer suggestions about the services, and keep posted about all operations concerning his companies. But he will have no work to perform beyond what he may wish to volunteer. The senior member will still do his job and the junior member his.

You have never heard of such an arrangement in business. But it works. The junior members are glad to put in extra time to have a share in that phase of the activities from which they have been excluded. The senior members and clients respect the contributions they make. You achieve better morale, lower turnover, and better understanding of the future potential of each member of the staff. Had you accepted any of the obvious answers, you would not have had the imaginative one pop out of your subconscious.

Much problem solving takes place in the subconscious. When it goes underground, we call it intuition. A significant part of the most imaginative solutions of the world's problems have been intuitive; yet intuition does not necessarily yield inspired or even satisfactory solutions. What is it, and how does it work?

Aunt Hannah was a great one for being right for the wrong reasons. "I wouldn't trust that Leo Bumwiler as far as I could see him," she would say. "He has those squinty eyes." Sure enough, next month Leo would be sent to the county jail for stealing a neighbor's ducks. Or she would say: "I wouldn't be surprised if Cousin Flora and the children came on from Missouri for a visit. There was a tall person and two short ones in my teacup this noon." A couple of days later Flora and the children would walk in. Aunt Hannah was not strong on logical procedures. But she could zero in on the right answer about as well as anyone I have ever known. We used to talk about Aunt Hannah's hunches. What she was using was intuition.

Have you not worked on a mathematics problem in vain for hours, gone to bed, and waked up with the answer neatly worked out? Have you not misplaced something, hunted high and low, and then days later recalled exactly where to find it? Have you not written a letter one morning and then before falling asleep had the correction of an error pop into your head unbidden? Intuition is not a branch of witchcraft. It is not even extrasensory perception. It is something with which you are equipped, and it is something that you can draw on. It is often called insight.

Intuition seems to be thinking speeded up to the nth degree. It is something like the new electronic brains that solve elaborate mathematical problems by scanning an unbelievable series of number combinations in a period of time infinitely less than the human brain can do the task. If you have ever seen a professional cryptographer break a coded message or even heard the panel of experts playing "Twenty Questions" on the radio, you have observed this speeded-up thinking in action. They scan their specialized data against the background of similar data stored in their minds. Your mind works the same way. When like Aunt Hannah you "instinctively" take a dislike to a person, your mind is scanning the accumulated experiences of your life. This accumulation includes both factual data and emotional prejudices. Your intuition, therefore, like an electronic computer is only as accurate as the data scanned and the machinery doing the scanning—your intelligence.

Only a sharp, formularized attack backed by a wealth of specialized experience can turn the jumble of letters and numbers of a cryptogram into a clear message or lead to the correct guess that someone is thinking about Old Mother Goose. A million random guesses probably would not yield the right answers. But even the most experienced logical attack is slow. Only intuition can twirl the dials of the mind fast enough to hit on the right answer within twenty questions or the brief time it takes a cryptographer to read a message in any ordinary code.

We commonly think that scientists solve their problems only by making logical deductions from laboriously accumulated experimental data. It is therefore almost shocking to have James Bryant Conant say, "The great working hypotheses of the past have rarely been the

product of careful examination of all facts and logical analysis."
Rather, he says, the origin of revolutionary scientific ideas is the
product of a "complex of intuition and logical reasoning." This position is abundantly supported by other scientists. We "elide the
preparation and the brooding," says William James. "When the
conclusion is there, we have already forgotten most of the steps pre-
ceding its attainment."

A little reading in the history of invention and reference to your
own experience will impress you with two facts. The first is: Intuition
solves only problems about which you know a lot. It is not reliable
outside of your own field of competence. Aunt Hannah has never had
a hunch that $E = Mc^2$. But I bet Aunt Hannah can beat any scientist when it comes to predicting what day Cousin Flora might
take it into her head to bring the kids on from Missouri for a surprise
visit. Aunt Hannah has given Cousin Flora, Leo Bumwiler, and all
her relatives and neighbors as close scrutiny over the years as Einstein
ever gave to mathematics and physics.

As with imagination, the second significant fact is: Intuitive solutions to difficult problems often occur in periods of relaxation or
change following periods of intense application to the problems. The
scholar-poet A. E. Housman described the mystery of his poetic
creation in this way: He would drink a pint of beer at lunch and
then walk for two or three hours, just observing nature. Unaccount-
ably a stanza or a line or two of verse would flow into his mind,
accompanied by a vague notion of what the whole poem would be.
After a lull "the spring would bubble up again." But usually the
completion of the final poem was a matter of later arduous conscious
addition and revision.

Under some conditions you have to use your intuition for immediate solutions. The physician looking at a desperately sick patient often has to make a life-and-death decision without time for
examination or tests of the usual sort. His intuition is based on
whatever signs his experience has taught him to note, whatever

181

analogies may be stored up in his memory. The executive, drawing on what Chester I. Barnard calls "persistent habitual experience," makes many an important decision with a speed that defies logical reconstruction. At a much less crucial level we all do every day.

To set the mechanism of imagination and intuition in motion, then, you must meet three conditions:

1. You have to be saturated in background knowledge of your problem.

2. You must concentrate on the problem (or similar problems) intensively for considerable time.

3. You must relax and turn aside from the problem.

Do not miss the significance of the obvious in this simple formula. Before the lightning of inspiration can strike you, before the solution can spring from the mysterious depths of your subconscious, before you can in any way count on nonlogical means to reach an answer that you have not been able to reach by logical processes, your mind must be made ready by uncommon intensity of thought about that problem. This intensive conditioning may go on for hours or for years. *Shropshire Lad* and Housman's two other slim volumes of poetry put into verse form ideas and feelings distilled from his whole life. From his boyhood until his death Thomas A. Edison thought of little else besides the problems connected with his inventions. When he was inventing the phonograph, he worked days and nights on end without going to bed.

On the other hand, the spark that produces the imaginative solution often jumps from experiences unrelated to the problem. Breadth of experience multiplies the sources of insight. Breadth of experience also acts to unify any series of experiences. From this unity, this understanding of the relatedness of a single problem to the large complex of which it is a part, imaginative answers arise more easily. Narrow specialization withers inspiration.

Since absorption in a single problem long enough to fill the mind with a comprehensive awareness of all its aspects is rare, it is no wonder that only the leaders in any field are visited by inspiration of a high order. On the other hand, some people who are considered lazy because they are not physically active have a way of finding the answers to the problems the busy workers of society find unsolvable. They work their minds longer and harder and with more concentration than busier people do.

A cautionary word: The fact that you may have arrived at your solution by intuition or any other nonlogical method does not relieve you of the obligation to defend it by logical means. "Oh, I don't know; I just have a hunch it will work" is not good enough.

In order to put your imagination and intuition to work, you can start by cultivating a creative attitude. You can assume a reserve toward obvious answers and a hospitality toward original ones. You can encourage the flow of fresh ideas by providing yourself with periods of idleness and periods of mechanical physical activity. Physical routine sometimes releases the imagination for creative purposes. More men have probably had inspirations while shaving than at any other time. Walking, chopping wood, running a lathe, and even washing dishes have proved productive. Lens-grinding must have been a singularly congenial occupation for the philosopher Spinoza. Monotonous physical activity sometimes crystallizes "the state of muddled suspense" that Whitehead says precedes successful creation. Some problem solvers seize their best solutions while listening to music. Others capture them while lying down—often just before falling asleep or waking fully.

You can occasionally hit on original solutions by conscious freewheeling—by taking your foot off the brake of routine and reason and allowing your mind to race. You then toss off ideas as fast as you can think them up, uninhibited by worries about what might be wrong with them. Among the wild, woolly, and indifferent solutions generated by this device is sometimes a winner, a diamond among the clinkers, that you would not be likely to discover by orthodox methods.

You may be able to carry on this technique best in a group with all members bouncing solutions back and forth as in a game of volleyball. On the other hand, you may find strolling about quiet streets or fields with a friend conducive to free and reciprocal speculation. When you are working on a problem alone, you may find it helpful to lie down to concentrate and to jot down your ideas as fast as they come to you.

If you are to practice problem solving as a creative art, you will use the imaginative approach as much as you do the logical. You will find a run-of-the-mill solution as repugnant as an illogical one. Whether you are trying to design a new milk container or a new fringe-benefits policy, you will query the obvious while you hunt for the ingenious and felicitous solution. You will experience few satisfactions sweeter than the one you get when you come up with an answer that goes beyond merely solving a problem and turns poor prospects into shining assets.

• • •

From your past record select your favorite examples of imaginative problem solving. Why do they seem original? Would you say that the principle of deviation from the norm is involved in each instance? Do you have a better explanation of originality? . . . Can you reconstruct the steps you followed in arriving at some of your imaginative solutions? . . . Choose a current problem where you believe an imaginative solution is in order. Decide on a norm—the obvious solution. The problem must be one that you are competent to solve, and it should be one that you have been studying intensively. Keep on studying it for as many hours and as many days as may be necessary. Keep the problem before you consciously as much as you can. Push it around. Write out as many solutions as you can think up. Read about it. Talk about it. Talk to a receptive companion as you walk in a quiet place. Try a freewheeling session with competent associates, with one acting as recorder while the rest toss out suggestions without inhibition. Then review the results. . . . Try the relaxing technique—lie down, listen to music of the Mozart and Haydn type, walk where you are not distracted by traffic or exertion, perform some easy monotonous task. . . . After several days, if you have not found a brilliant solution, you should at least have a better one than you started with. Adopt that temporarily, if you can, and let your intuition take it from there.

22

Calculated Risk

❧ *The cows were all healthy* ❧

PROFESSIONAL baseball players talk about playing "percentage ball." With the score 1–0 in the third inning and a man on first base, percentage ball dictates that the next batter will bunt. He will probably be thrown out, but he will advance the other runner to second base, in a position to score with the tying run. Here the professional thing to do is to play it safe—to try merely to even the score. In more desperate situations, percentage ball calls for the hit and run, home run, or other long chance. At such times a bunt would be as unorthodox as a long ball in the first situation. The unorthodox here is more reckless than imaginative, for it reduces the probability of success. Calculating the risk shrewdly is what makes a pro. He plays percentage ball.

You cannot solve problems, any more than you can play baseball, without taking risks. It is the professional thing to make your decisions on a percentage basis. You choose the solution that seems to offer the highest percentage in your favor. Only in the wonder world of mathematics do problems have perfect solutions. In the normal situations which you face you cannot hope for perfect answers. You cannot even hope to be positive that you have chosen the best of the possible answers. You can only accept—or reject—the belief that it is wise to play percentage ball. It is wise to put your faith in those

186

solutions that experience shows produce satisfactory answers most often.

Baseball players and gamblers are not the only people who are concerned about odds. For instance, the entire structure of insurance rests on actuarial mathematics. Actuaries calculate the odds against your dying inconveniently soon or your house burning down within the year and then figure the premiums you have to pay accordingly. Odds equal the ratio between favorable and unfavorable alternatives.

Are you not running your life on a percentage basis? You do not know for sure that if you spend several years studying law or pharmacy you will be able to make a good living. You do not know for sure that if you marry Eloise you will be happy. You do not know for sure that you will live long enough to get your full return from the retirement fund you contribute to each month. But you act as though you did. In each case you think the odds are good enough for you to take a chance.

So you solve your problems on a percentage basis. Long-odds solutions may in fact work very well. But you bet on the solutions that *probably* will work more often than others. Hitler's fantastic hunches sometimes paid off, but in the long run he was defeated because he could not provide effective answers to enough of the problems that overwhelmed him.

How in a given situation can you figure out the probability of success? Perhaps that is your toughest problem. You have to figure out your percentage in regard to each problem in its specific circumstances.

When the Garrets moved to a town out in the country, their neighbors recommended Mr. Easthill, a farmer, as a supplier of chickens, eggs, butter, milk, and cream. The Garrets found the milk and cream and butter brought back happy childhood recollections, and the prices were wonderfully low.

Then a neighbor who had had undulant fever for seven years

dropped in. The Garrets talked to a doctor. Yes, there were cases of undulant fever in the town off and on, and it came from diseased cows. Pasteurizing was the best safeguard. Some of the Garrets' friends and Mr. Easthill pooh-poohed their fears. Mr. Easthill admitted that the milk was not pasteurized, but it was perfectly safe. The cows were all healthy, and their stables and all the equipment were kept as clean as could be. Hundreds of families in the area had been raised on unpasteurized milk. The Garrets thought the matter over and made their decision: The odds against their contracting undulant fever might be a million to one, but the consequences—seven years of illness, perhaps—far outweighed the pleasures of rich yellow cream and low prices.

You are driving through a state you do not know well—West Virginia, say—where large towns are few. When you come to acceptable overnight accommodations early in the evening, you decide to stop. It is wiser to sacrifice the final hour or so of daylight than to gamble on finding quarters later. Your second stop might not be nearly so acceptable, and you might have to drive until you are exhausted to find even that.

One of the simplest ways for you to solve problems by playing percentage ball is to do what there is to do. What does that mean? In many situations action seems hopeless. The odds against the successful outcome of any one of the apparent solutions of the problem confronting you may seem too overwhelming for you to make a move. But doing nothing *is* action. It is negative action, but it is a commitment—a decision. And doing nothing has consequences just as surely as doing something has. The small consequences of doing something may still create an opening for further positive moves.

The captain of a merchant vessel heading for the safety of one of the Pacific islands during the early months of World War II learned that the island was occupied by the Japanese. He knew that elements of the Japanese fleet were on the other side of him. East of him was Japan-controlled Asia. Wracked by doubt, he cruised slowly in a circle, a sitting duck for enemy subs or planes. After forty-eight hours without sleep, he began to lose his grip on himself as well as the situation. His executive officer took over the command, set a course in the least threatening direction, and boldly sailed the ship to safety.

Many a youth sending out letters of application for a job has wondered after a few rebuffs why he should send out any more. Many a salesman trudging from store to store has wondered why he should make even one more call. Many a beginning writer has wondered why he should spend postage sending his MS. to another editor and risk another rejection slip. In all of these instances and in all like them doing what there is to do inevitably increases the percentage favorably. The increase may seem imperceptible. But .001 per cent is better odds than .00 per cent. So long as you can make a positive move, you make it.

Let us have no misunderstanding. It is wise not to solve any problems that you do not have to solve. Save your time, your nerves, and your brains until you are certain that a problem exists and that you are the person who has to do the solving. Many problems, like storms, never arrive in spite of threatening skies. Part of your standard technique must be to wait and see. When one does arrive, it may be so different from the one you thought was coming that any anticipatory efforts would have been wasted. Then, too, it may have someone else's name written on it. Wait and see.

A decision must sometimes be made on the basis of preferring relatively known odds to unknown odds. General Eisenhower made the most important decision of the war on this basis.

After the greatest single military action in history, the invasion of Europe, had begun in the English ports, it was halted for twenty-four hours because of bad weather. The weather experts predicted a slight temporary improvement on the following day and then worse weather for an indefinite period. While LST's and the rest of the invasion fleet rolled in the rough seas and the tightly packed troops became ill by the thousands, the General sweated out his historic decision through the bitter hours.

In his battle headquarters Eisenhower wrestled with the problem of going ahead with the invasion and risking the chance that worsening weather might cause a major catastrophe or of waiting at least two weeks and taking a chance on greater German alertness and on totally unknown factors of the weather at that time. He made the fateful decision to go ahead. The weather over the Channel abated enough to make the crossing possible, and the decision to cross in such weather caught the enemy by surprise.

The decisiveness of General Eisenhower, his judgment in weighing the factors in the situation, and his courage in taking the responsibility for acting on the basis of what seemed the better odds, gave the Allies a spectacular and relatively bloodless beachhead for the invasion. Unwillingness to act would have led to delay that might have stretched to a year before propitious weather conditions returned, during which Hitler would have been destroying England with his buzz bombs and jet planes and making his coastal defenses stronger, perhaps impregnable.

No example can better illustrate the principle of the calculated risk. Whenever your solution of a problem has a high degree of probability of succeeding, you do not have much of a problem. The real problems of life, both personal and professional, are full of uncertainty. All solutions, no matter how painstakingly reached or how well grounded on experience, are vulnerable. The variables in any situation can throw off the percentage and change success to failure. Had the wind blown ten or twenty miles an hour harder on June 6, 1944, history undoubtedly would have recorded one of its greatest failures. The Invincible Armada that Philip II sent from Spain in 1588 for the invasion of Britain suffered a historic defeat, largely because of weather.

Professor Victor Goedicke kindly provides the following simplified explanation of mathematical expectation on which calculated risk depends: "Statisticians define 'probability' as the ratio f/n, where f is the number of possible favorable outcomes and n is the total number of possible outcomes. For example, a standard roulette wheel contains eighteen red numbers, eighteen black numbers, and two other numbers. The probability that red will turn up is therefore 18/38. Statisticians then define mathematical expectation as 'winnings times probability of winning.' If a man bets $10 on red, his expectation is the amount he will receive if he wins $20 times his probability of winning (18/38). This amounts to about $9.47. This is the cash value of his bet as soon as he has placed it. He has, in short, spent $10 to buy $9.47 worth of merchandise and has thrown away 53¢. If he makes a long series of such bets, he can expect to lose an average of about 53¢ per bet. Expectation is the best rational evaluation of your equity in an uncompleted gambling operation. Every decision you make in life requires that you evaluate the worth of an uncompleted gambling operation; this is almost a definition of life."

Professor Goedicke continues: "If the Garrets applied this technique to their calculated risk, they could be more confident of their conclusion. If there had been, for example, three cases of undulant fever out of three thousand people who drank unpasteurized milk, then the probability of getting undulant fever from unpasteurized milk is 3/3000 or one in a thousand, not one in a million. If furthermore Garret estimates that seven years' illness is worth $50,000 in loss of earnings and medical costs, then he can compute that his 'expectation' of loss is 1/1000 times $50,000 or $50. This is too much to pay for the pleasure of drinking a glass of milk."

All problem solving of any significance, therefore, must be understood as having the character of a calculated risk. The nature of many problems makes impossible the gathering of sufficient data for an easy decision or for much certainty about the outcome of the decision. All marriages belong in this category. Many other problems have time limits that make decision and action imperative before all the data can be collected and weighed or all the people consulted who ought to be consulted. If Eisenhower had waited for better weather, the tides on the Normandy beach would have been unsatisfactory for landing operations. The whole gigantic, complicated operation of the invasion was bracketed within forty-eight hours or so when for an hour or two at high tide the landing was possible. Men of action take a dim view of columnists, professors, and other Monday morning quarterbacks because they so generally fail to appreciate the way the problem looked at the time the decision had to be made.

The art of an expert chef is often said to lie in the subtlety of his seasoning. Risk is the seasoning in problem solving, and your craft as a problem solver lies in the subtlety with which you estimate the risk in a given course of action. To calculate risk skilfully demands experience and intelligence, but it also demands the flexibility of spirit that in all fields distinguishes the artist from the less inspired.

•   •   •

Cast your mind back over your problem-solving record. Do you play percentage ball consistently? Does your ratio of satisfactory and unsatisfactory solutions show that you calculate your risk with skill? Does it suggest that you take unnecessary chances? Or are you too cautious? . . . Review each important decision that you are about to make. Have you assembled enough data on which to base each decision? Have you studied the data carefully enough? Have you analyzed each step in the light of your reading in *The Art of Problem Solving?* Will making a decision now be better than not making one? Of the several possible solutions, which is the safest? Which will yield the maximum results? In separate columns list the favorable and the unfavorable factors. How do you now rate the probability of your success? Do you still think your decision represents a reasonable calculated risk? Are you able to express your probability of success statistically? . . . Do you now find problem solving fun? Is it an art?

23

Summing Up

LEARNING to solve problems is like learning to play baseball. You learn to throw, to catch, to bat, to run bases, to make plays, and to execute all sorts of refinements of these basic skills. You do not learn to play baseball. You learn these basic skills separately, and you put them together in new combinations every game. So in this final word I repeat what I said in the first chapter: There is no one-two-three method for solving problems. You learn the skills, and you combine them to play the game as circumstances dictate.

What actually occurs in the process of solving problems? And how can you use this book to help you?

Do you not have to meet two general situations? The first is the new problem—one which you may or may not settle with normal effort. The other is one that after normal effort still has you stumped. What happens as you deal with these two types of problems?

A new problem will take varying amounts of time and degrees of conscious use of the material you and I have gone over. You solve some new problems instantaneously. You take in their essence at once, and through experience, intuition, or chance you hit on a satisfactory answer right away. You solve other new problems in an unpredictable sequence of steps. Normally, you start with recognition of a problem situation—something is wrong. You limit that to

194

what specifically is wrong—the essential diagnosis of the problem (often mistaken). The sequence breaks here. Your experience with similar problems will usually determine your attack. You may gather data, or you may analyze the data and issues already present. You may then see a promising alternative. You try it, and it works. Or it does not work. Then you check your facts or your assumptions and find your trouble. Or you go on making the moves that seem appropriate until, with what you think of as a normal amount of effort, you have your solution. You will rarely follow exactly the same sequence twice.

What happens when you are stumped? Then you will review with much more conscious awareness the various aspects of problem solving that we have considered. Perhaps with a tough problem in the foreground of your mind you will browse through this book. As you read, you may ask yourself: "Am I making an assumption that is not true? Are my facts accurate? Is there an alternative I have not thought of? Can I restructure this problem in some way? Can I break the deadlock by trying out a solution on an experimental basis? Is there a logical fallacy buried in my reasoning? Am I being fooled by any cause-and-effect relations? Is there a bold fresh way of attacking this problem?" These and a multitude of similar questions you will ask yourself about your persistent problems. Perhaps you will find one answer and end your troubles. Perhaps you will get an idea that will enable you to make a positive move that may lead to other moves and a temporary or final solution.

Your whole effort as a problem solver is directed at increasing your mathematical expectations of favorable results. You reduce the risk by increasing your skill in calculating. Your early efforts to master the art of oil painting, say, are frustrating because of your sudden realization of the amazing extent of the color combinations at your disposal. So at first you may feel inhibited by your awareness of the various aspects of problem solving that we have thought about together. But as in painting, with practice your self-consciousness will

195

give way to assurance. Then you will have this tremendous advantage: You will be able to bring to bear on your problems not only your knowledge of the specific content of a problem but also your knowledge of the nature of problems in general. Then you will experience that esthetic pleasure that makes problem solving an art.

Index

[*Note:* ex. refers to examples used in text.]

Accuracy, 42, 45-48
Additives, 95, 98-99
Admiral of the Ocean Sea, 149
Alternatives, 59-65; dilemma, 63-64; doing nothing, 59-60, 62; either-or, 62-63; multiple, 64
Ambiguity, 22, 25
Amelioration, 5, 12
Analogy, 141-148; correspondence as, 142; historical approach as, 146; hypotheses from, 143-144; legal precedents as, 146; sampling as, 144-145; by unit and phase, 145-146
Analysis, 25-32; alphabetical, 25; chronological, 28; by classification, 28-29; from concrete to abstract, 28; by difficulty, 28; by issues, 30; by key factors, 29; by key words, 30; by logical structure, 26-27; numerical, 27-28; by significance, 30-31; visual aids to, 25
Anthropology, 53
Antigone ex., 63
Anxiety ex., 19
Apology, 41
Archimedes, 23
Aristotle, 34, 163
Armstrong, Duff, ex., 49
Arnold, Thurman, 52
Art, problem solving as, 161
Assumptions, 39, 51-55; challenging, 51, 55; faulty, 52-53; hidden, 54; social, 53-54
Attack, 57
Authorities, 47-48

Automobile shows ex., 40, 175
Auxiliaries, 94-101; additive, 95, 98-99; equivalence, 95-96; neutral or zero factor, 95, 99-100; substitution, 95-97; X-factor, 101
Awareness, 175-176, 182

Bach, Johann Sebastian, 176
Bacon, Francis, 147
Baer, Karl Ernst von, 113
Baker, John C., 34
Barnard, Chester I, 103-104, 182
Basement waterproofing ex., 77
Beer bottle label ex., 30
Berenson, Bernard, 81
Bill sorter ex., 18-19, 22
Blanket sales ex., 29-30
Blood circulation ex., 33
Boy and dog ex., 44
Brick terrace ex., 98
Bridge building ex., 5
Budget ex., 31-32
Burke, Edmund, 30
"Burr" puzzle ex., 124-125

Cafeteria ex., 88-89
Calculated risk, 186-193; doing nothing, 188; mathematical expectation, 191; odds, 187-189; "percentage ball," 186-187; probability, 5-6; 136, 139, 187, 190-191; statistics, 191
Car collision ex., 49
Car keys ex., 125
Cardozo, Benjamin, 120
Cause and effect, 149-160; association, consistency of, 158; criteria, 151-152; hidden causes, 155-156; "Post hoc ergo propter hoc," 156-157;

197

INDEX

198

INDEX

99-100; strength and weakness of, 69-70; T-, 80; weighing, 67-68; X-, 101

Facts, 42-50; accuracy of, 42, 45-48; checking, 46-48; and fiction, 44; memory of, 49; and opinion, 44, 49-50; recognition of, 43-44, 46, 50; significance of, 43

Failure, 23, 75

Fatigue ex., 155-156

"Feedback," 167

Fiction, 44

Figures, diagrams, and symbols, 18, 23, 25, 29, 95-96

Financial reorganization ex., 46-47

Finlay, Dr. Carlos Juan, 126

Fisherman's boat ex., 103

Follett, Mary Parker, 168

Food for hogs ex., 127

Formula, 86-93; abstracting a, 90; closed-system, 91; custom as, 91-92; as efficiency, 87; habit as, 87; rigidity of, 90; schematizing as, 89; systems of thought as, 91

Franklin, Benjamin, 120

Fraternity ex., 152-153

Free enterprise, 128

Free-wheeling, 183-184

Fromm, Erich, 115

Furnace ex., 51

Furniture in barracks ex., 174

Galilei, Galileo, 76, 176

GE Creative Engineering, 176

Genius, 176

Gestalt theory, 31-32

Gilbert and Sullivan, 133

Glen Cove, N. Y., police, 60-61

Goats in Near East ex., 69

Goedicke, Victor, 124-125, 190-191

Goudy, Frederic W., 171

Grimaldi, John U., 156

Grimm, Jacob, 117

Gutenberg, Johann, 76

Habit, 3, 87, 166

Hamilton, Alexander, 105

Harvard Medical School, 115

Harvey, Dr. William, 33, 113

Hasty generalization, 137

Hayes, Roland, 94

Heifetz, Jascha, 171

High-school prom ex., 15, 20, 22

Hippocrates, 113

Hiring engineer ex., 105

History, 85, 146

History of language ex., 117

Hitler, Adolph, 187

Hooke, Robert, 115

House buying ex., 67-68

Housewives' ailments ex., 26

Housing projects ex., 73

Housman, A. E., 181, 182

How We Think, 3

Hughes, Charles Evans, 48

Hurricane ex., 59-60

Hypothesis, 113-121; from analogy, 143-144; basis for, 117; and conceptual schemes, 116; in experiments, 125-126, 128; inclusiveness of, 116; and law, 115; multiple, 118; and speculation, 115-119; as strategy, 119; testing, 119-120; and theory, 115-116, 119-120; working, 116

Identification, 11-17; of real problem, 12-14; of total problem, 14-17

Imagination, 171-185; absorption and, 172-173, 182; awareness of needs and, 175-176; breadth of experience and, 182; control of, 176; encouraging the, 183-184; genius and, 176; and intuition, 178-183; and knowledge, 172; and obvious, 173-174; and originality, 172

Imitation, 165

Induction, 132, 135-138

Inferences, 44; see Logic

Inspiration, 173, 182-183

Intersection ex., 153-155

Intuition, 178-183; concentration and, 181-182; encouraging, 183-184; insight as, 180; and knowledge, 181-182; relaxation and, 181-182; subconscious in, 178

199

INDEX

Invasion of Europe ex., 189-190
Issues, 30

James, William, 181
Japanese bases ex., 61-62
Job change ex., 1, 64
Johnson, Wendell, 37
Jungle clearing ex., 27

Kelvin, William T., 1st Baron, 45
Kettering, Charles F., 155, 168
Know-how, 165
Knowns, 21-22

Law, 49-50, 115, 146
Law school Senior ex., 138
Leather business ex., 89-90
Leeuwenhoek, Anton van, 55
Leonardo da Vinci, 176
Leverage ex., 164
Lewin, Kurt, 82
Library ex., 60
Libraries, 48, 167
Liebig, Justus, Baron von, 117
Lincoln, Abraham, 35-36, 49, 102-103
Linnaeus (Karl von Linné), 28
Lippershey, Hans, 176
Logic, 5-6, 53, 130-140; deductive, 132-134; inductive, 135-138; inductive-deductive, 138-139
Logical-mindedness, 139
Loss-gain, 72
Louisiana purchase ex., 63
Lyell, Sir Charles, 42

MacArthur, Douglas, 61-62
Machine operator ex., 45
Magellan, Ferdinand, 135
Manufacturer's wife ex., 88
Market prices ex., 136, 137
Marshall, George C., 75
Martin, Harold H., 97
Mathematical expectation, 191
McClellan, George B., 35, 36
Meade, George G., 102-103
Measurement, 45
Medical mission ex., 74
Medical oil ex., 144

Mediocrity, 173-174
Memory, 49, 164-165
Mental hospital ex., 150, 156-157
Merchant vessel ex., 188-189
Microscope ex., 55
Migraine headache ex., 127
Morgan, Thomas Hunt, 135
Morgenthau plan ex., 13
Morison, Samuel E., 149
Moving day ex., 88
Murder mystery ex., 118-119
Murderers in Papua ex., 174
Murray, Sir Hubert, 174
Mushrooms ex., 134

Napoleon I, 63, 79
Newton, Sir Isaac, 76, 173
New York Times, 60
Nitrogen ex., 53
Non-logical methods, 183; see Imagination
November offensive ex., 66-67

Oak tree ex., 62-63
Odds, 187-189
Office building ex., 79-80
Office machine ex., 16
Office manager ex., 11
Office supplies ex., 87
Omaha beach ex., 48
Opaque projector ex., 29
Opinion, 44, 49-50; see Logic
Originality, 172
Overweight ex., 116

Pascal, Blaise, 22
Pasteur, Louis, 117
Patent release ex., 128
Patience, 84
"Percentage ball," 186-187
Perfectionists, 64
Piano ex., 95
Plato, 34, 41
Poetry composing ex., 181
Point of view, 103, 108-109
Polya, G., 107
Porgy, 48
"Post hoc ergo propter hoc," 156-157

INDEX

Preconceived notions, 54
Predictability; see Probability
Price increases *ex.*, 75, 83-84
Prince, Wood, 97
Printing business *ex.*, 14
Probability, 5-6, 136, 139, 187, 190-191
Problems; changing, 6, 16; complexity of, 6; concept of, 15; defined, 3-4; difficult, 194; in future, 13, 15, 39, 80-81, 84, 150; new, 194; real, 12-14; record of, 7; talking over, 11-12, 19-21, 49, 184; total, 14-17, 72
Problem situation, 4, 11-12, 23, 92
Problem solving; aspects of, 2-3, 9, 57, 111, 161; attitude, 35; as calculated risk, 191-192; conferences, 38; criteria for, 77-78; importance of, 1; steps in, 3
Publishing house *ex.*, 62
Purdue University, 127
Purkinje, J. E., 29
Purpose, change of, 104-105

Questionnaires, 39-40
Questions, 33-41; directional, 37; formulating, 33-34, 36; key, 36; leading, 37; precise, 37; restatement of, 39; terminology of, 36-37

Radio cabinet *ex.*, 73-74
Rask, Rasmus, 117
Rayleigh, John W. S., 3d Baron, 52
Reading, 48, 85
Real problem, 12-14
Rearrangement of factors, 105-108
Reasoning; see Logic
Records of problems, 7, 23, 167
Reed, Dr. Walter, 126
Relativity, 6
Relaxation, 181-182
Renoir, Jean, 173
Renoir, Pierre Auguste, 173
Resources, 167
Restatement, 15, 22-23, 39
Restaurant space *ex.*, 86
Restructuring, 102 - 109; through change of point of view, 103, 108-

109; through change of purpose, 104-105; by rearranging factors, 105-108
Revolutionary War *ex.*, 152
Rigidity, 90
Rivitz, Hiram, 79
Roethlisberger, F. J., 163
Roosevelt, Franklin D., 85
Roulette *ex.*, 191
Russia *ex.*, 15

Sampling, 125-127, 144-146
Sales techniques *ex.*, 145
Saturday Evening Post, 97
Schliemann, Heinrich, 114
School budget *ex.*, 81
Scientific approach, 111
Scientific methods, 45
Scientific spirit, 45, 129
Semantics, 22
Shakespeare, William, 175
Shropshire Lad, 182
Sick wife *ex.*, 12
Signs, 157-159
Skepticism, 34, 47, 55
Snakes *ex.*, 44
Socrates, 34
Solutions; defined, 4-5; criteria for, 77-78; new problems caused by, 72-73; obvious, 173; statement of, 23
Speculation, 115, 119, 184
Spinoza, Baruch, 183
State highway patrol *ex.*, 88
Statement of problems, 18-24; figures, diagrams, and symbols, use of, in, 23; knowns, unknowns, and what is sought in, 21-22; oral, 19-21, 184; and restatement, 22-23; semantics and, 22; and solutions, 23; written, 21
Statistics, 46, 120, 191
Stimson, Henry L., 85
Stock yards *ex.*, 97
Stouffer, Vernon, 86
Strategy, 119
Subconscious, the, 178-183
Substitution, 95, 96-97
Sumner, William G., 166

201

INDEX